MW01041476

The Paths We Walk

Trails

FELICIA FERGUSON

WestBow Press books may be ordered through booksellers or by contacting:

WestBow Press
A Division of Thomas Nelson & Zondervan
1663 Liberty Drive
Bloomington, IN 47403
www.westbowpress.com
1 (866) 928-1240

ISBN: 978-1-5127-6120-7 (sc)
ISBN: 978-1-5127-6121-4 (hc)
ISBN: 978-1-5127-6119-1 (e)

Library of Congress Control Number: 2016917399

Print information available on the last page.

WestBow Press rev. date: 10/21/2016

To my own small-group ladies, Kendall, Sarah,
Melissa, Hannah, Kim, and Shelley.
May you be blessed one-thousand fold for
your friendship and inspiration.

With thanks to Anne, my Fairhope tour guide and font of wisdom,
Mindi, my sounding board for all things psychological,
and Gary, for teaching me how to meditate biblically.

Chapter 1

Fairhope

The ping was ordinary and not unexpected by any of the four very busy ladies. E-mails regularly entered their inboxes and were read and deleted or saved and pondered as the need dictated. However, this e-mail, while disappointing in its contents, would lead to more changes than any of them would have dreamed. In fact, it was an e-mail that would change everything.

Anne Greeley stood in the hallway of a doctor's office with a box of client files propped on one hip. She tugged her phone out of her purse at the sound of her incoming e-mail swoosh. Expecting it to be an announcement from her employer about a new drug in their pharmaceutical lineup, she was surprised to see it was from the church. She frowned as she thumbed open the e-mail. The ladies' Bible study wasn't due to start for another two weeks, and she wasn't on any other church e-mail list, preferring to get her information from the bulletin or the webpage since it was on her work account.

"Oh no!" she gasped as she read the e-mail. Muriel Hartwig, who had led the Bible study for the past three years, had had an emergency bypass surgery after going to the ER with chest pains the night before. Anne figured the lady's age to be around sixty, given that all of the study participants except herself and three others were in their late fifties or older. The ladies' Bible study was being placed on hold while Muriel recovered, which also left the fall retreat up in the air since that group had always organized and hosted it.

Anne said a quick prayer for Muriel's smooth transition from the hospital to rehab and then later home. She hated that Muriel was in pain and wished her all the best. The older lady was the reason Anne now had three of her closest friends. Jess, Lindsay, Deli, and Anne all attended the same church but either in different services or, in Deli's case, so intermittently due to work obligations, they wouldn't recognize one another, especially given Deli's frequently changing hair color.

Muriel's Bible study brought them all together on Tuesday nights. In spite of their differing marital statuses, work histories, and interests, the four ladies, all in their late thirties, had become fast friends and met at least once a month—or whenever their schedules allowed—for coffee or even a girls' afternoon. Anne would be forever indebted to Muriel and her Bible study.

She knew the other three would be as surprised as she. Thumbing over to her text message app, Anne sent out a group text to her friends.

Heartened by the instant camaraderie, Anne tucked her phone back into her purse and pushed open the office door, ready to answer questions and to stock sample supplies.

~~*

Jess McAdams, the volunteer coordinator of The Hospital at Fairhope, slipped through the crowded registration area bustling with patients checking in for procedures, appointments, or hospital stays. She scooted into an elevator just as the door was closing, greeted the older couple in the elevator with a smile, and pressed the button for the fourth floor. She noticed the already lit button for the third floor, which housed labor and delivery. *They must be new grandparents or even great-grandparents. What a blessing for their family!* she thought with a smile.

Jess would love to have a family of her own, and at thirty-seven, could hear the clock ticking. It apparently was loud enough that her boyfriend of three years, Mitch, overheard it. He was beginning to make broad hints about getting married. Mitch was a great guy who had a good job and a solid family background. He would be a good husband and father, and he loved her very much. She knew she should be overjoyed that he was ready for the next step—but she wasn't.

It wasn't that Jess didn't love him. She did, deeply. She would love to grow old with Mitch holding her hand. They fit well together, and she could see them as husband and wife in all respects—except the one that was most important: their faith. They had both grown up in church, but whereas she had developed an abiding love for God, Mitch had learned to grin and bear Him. Age and experience hadn't changed his opinion, but it had deepened hers.

The elevator dinged, heralding the older couple's floor, and Jess stepped to the side to allow them plenty of room to exit. As the doors closed, she watched a young man wrap the woman in a bear hug. *Must be the new dad,* Jess thought with a fond smile, and then she turned her thoughts to the reason for leaving her office.

Muriel Hartwig had arrived at the ER the night before with chest pains and had been promptly whisked into an OR for an emergency bypass. At sixty-two, she had the energy of a woman half her age and the appetite of a born-and-raised Southerner. Jess wasn't surprised to hear that the years of biscuits and gravy, fried chicken, and sweet tea had finally caught up with her.

The elevator dinged again, and Jess exited. The fourth floor was divided into the heart and stroke wings, with the ICU in the middle. She glanced into a vacant room as she turned left. Her mother had died in that hospital, and her room on the cancer wing of the second floor was set up much the same as those on this floor. It was odd, but working there didn't bother Jess at all. In fact, she felt closer to her mother at the hospital than anywhere else. Amid the astringents and iodine, she would occasionally catch a whiff of her mother's perfume. Even through the months of chemo and later hospice care, Jenna McAdams, ever the Southern lady, always put on her full face. It just wasn't done otherwise.

Jess smiled as she reached the room of the lady who had become, if not a surrogate mother, at least a very wise aunt. That very wise aunt's eyes brightened as she spied Jess in the doorway. "Please, come in, Jess!" she said, struggling to come to a sitting position.

Jess rushed to her bedside to stay the motion. "Not yet, Muriel! Use the remote, and lift the head of the bed."

Muriel shook her head, banishing the last vestiges of the anesthesia-induced fog. "You'll have to forgive me, dear. I'm not accustomed to the sickbed."

Jess patted her arm fondly and replied, "You'll be up and at 'em in no time, I'm sure. How are you feeling today? I was surprised not to have to force my way through the throng of visitors."

Muriel chuckled. "I'm sure they're just waiting for the doctor to drop the flag, and then it'll be pedal to the metal," she said without recrimination. NASCAR was second only to the Bible in Muriel's list of favorite things. Jess sighed inwardly. She wished Mitch had those priorities, but she was certain that Alabama football would always be number one in his heart.

"Hey, what's this? Why the long face?"

Caught in her rumination of things she couldn't change, Jess blushed. "Sorry, Muriel, I just drifted for a moment."

Muriel shot her a sharp look. "Thinking about that young man of yours?"

Jess glanced away, a trace of guilt furrowing her brow. *What is wrong with me? I should be comforting Muriel, not the other way around.* Inwardly castigating herself for her lack of manners, she pulled out the brightest smile from her normally cheery disposition bag and turned back. "In a way, yes, but let's talk about you. What did Dr. Hall say?"

Muriel looked concerned at the abrupt change of topic. Jess thought she must suspect that all was not sunshine and roses in that quarter; but, bless her, the older lady answered the question without any more of her own. "Well, he said what he's been telling me for years," she cackled. "No more of my favorite foods, or I will get to meet my Jesus sooner than He probably planned!"

Jess nodded. "I was wondering about that. Muriel, you have to start taking care of yourself. There are too many people who love and would miss you. Has the dietician been in yet to discuss anything?"

"I expect her to bear the bad news sometime today. Ah, me." She sighed and adjusted the sheet over her rotund form. "I've known this was coming, but it's hard to change a lifetime's habits and preferences."

"Well, think of it as you having other things you would rather do than be stuck in here," Jess teased.

A knock at the door turned Jess in its direction. She flashed a welcoming smile to greet the newcomer. "Rachel, we were just talking about you!"

Muriel grinned. "So you're the hatchet man—or rather, woman?"

Rachel pushed her long, dark bangs behind her ear and chuckled. "If you mean the person who is going to take away your fried foods, then yes."

Jess patted Muriel's hand and said, "I'll leave you two to talk."

Muriel placed her hand on Jess's to stay her a moment, and Jess knew Muriel hadn't forgotten their earlier conversation. "My dear," she whispered, "if you're having any doubts at all about your young man, don't do anything in a hurry. It's best to wait until you have peace."

Jess blinked back the sudden tears and offered a wan smile of thanks. "We'll talk again soon, Muriel." She rose, and Rachel took her place at Muriel's bedside.

Jess paused at the door to gather herself before potentially meeting coworkers or volunteers under her direction. "Peace," Muriel had said.

But that was the question. Would she ever have peace without a change in Mitch's faith?

She had so looked forward to the return of the Bible study and the women's retreat, needing some of the insight she always gained from her older sisters in the faith. Unfortunately, it appeared that door had closed. It was doubtful that anyone would want to take up the reins in Muriel's stead for either the study or the retreat, given her years of tenure in both positions.

Jess squared her shoulders and put aside her reflections. There were others there who had greater needs to tend to than her ambivalent heart. As she walked out the door, she found two of her floor volunteers, needing direction for the afternoon. Grateful for the distraction, she happily answered each question and assigned their duties.

~~*

Lindsay Davenport stepped into the deliciously cool Southern Floral Designs. Although the calendar said it was the end of August, the heat hadn't taken the hint and begun its customary leave of absence. A moment later, she was warmly greeted with a smile from the store's floral designer, Jerry.

Two years before, John had surprised her with a bouquet of flowers from the florist for her thirty-seventh birthday. The arrangement Jerry had created was stunning in its use of cabbage roses, peonies, and baby's breath. Lindsay had used Southern Floral ever since for any floral needs.

Refrigerators filled with a variety of premade arrangements, each lovely in its own right, lined one wall. A few free-standing tables laden with small gifts filled the center of the room. With a friendly nod and a "Hi, Jerry," Lindsay moved to get a closer look at the ready-made arrangements.

Jerry came out from behind the counter and met her. "So I'm guessing you've heard about Muriel, then?"

Lindsay nodded. "I need something to take to her on behalf of myself and some friends. I don't suppose there's an arrangement that hasn't made it up to her room already, is there?"

Jerry chuckled then scratched his forehead above the eye patch that covered his right eye. Lindsay had no idea what had happened to the eye and figured she didn't know him well enough to ask. "Well," he answered, "I'm thinking the carnations and the tea roses are still up for grabs, but then if you want something she can keep for later, we have a pretty bird of paradise that's just about to pop."

Normally, Lindsay would love to purchase something that could be planted and enjoyed for years on end. However, she wasn't certain how long Muriel would be in the hospital and later her cardiac therapy, and she didn't want to put an added responsibility of caring for a plant on the older lady. "Hmm, I think I need to stick with the ones that won't need long-term care."

Jerry nodded. "Probably not a bad idea."

"But these, as pretty as they are, aren't really speaking to me. What flowers do you have in stock, and do you have time to put something together for me now? I hate to ask, but I want to drop them off personally, and I have to pick up the girls from school to get them to dance and—"

He put up his hands at the verbal onslaught. Abashed, Lindsay shook her head and eased back on her type-A overdrive.

Jerry offered an understanding smile. "I've got just the thing in the back. I know how much you love cabbage roses, and I have a bouquet of yellow ones I've almost finished. Why don't you take a look?" He stepped into his design room behind the counter and returned with a display of yellow cabbage roses offset with greenery, wood, and a hint of baby's breath.

"Oh, Jerry, that's perfect just as it is! What do you mean you haven't finished it?"

The tips of his ears pinked at the praise, but he cleared his throat and answered, "I had planned to add a pop of a lily or two, but I'm more than willing to let you have it as is."

"Oh, do! Muriel will love this." Lindsay pulled out her wallet, offered her credit card, and then selected a get well card from the display in front of the register. She signed all four ladies' names to the card and her own to the receipt, then tucked the card in the arrangement and turned to leave. With a hurried "Thank you so much, Jerry!" she was out the door and back in her SUV. A quick glance at the clock revealed she would have time for a short visit with Muriel before needing to leave for the elementary school.

However, when she arrived at the nurses' station on Muriel's floor, the shift nurse informed her that Muriel was resting after having her first post-surgery physical therapy session. Lindsay shot a look of sympathy toward Muriel's room and asked for the flowers to be delivered whenever it was appropriate and to let Muriel know she had stopped by. The nurse assured her she would, and Lindsay returned to her car. She looked at the clock again. There was just enough time to get the girls from school, change them into their leotards, and head to the dance studio. *Where has the day gone?* she thought.

~~*

Anne parked her Audi SUV by the neighborhood's cluster mailboxes, cut the engine, and pulled out her box key. The kids would be getting off the bus in about an hour, which gave her just enough time to get the mail, change out of her work clothes, and begin thinking about supper. In the foreground she could see a foursome chatting on the ninth hole.

When she and Ted had first married, they had opted for a condo rather than a house since they had neither the money for a huge down payment nor the time for the upkeep of a large yard. Now, more than ten years later, their condo's price per square foot had more than doubled, which made it one of their better investments. Ever better than that, though, was the location. She loved looking out at the water as she walked along Battles Wharf every morning. It was the most peaceful place for her devotionals.

Anne tugged at the magazines and junk mail that overflowed their mail slot. She made a mental note to once again call and cancel the unsolicited magazines that appeared out of nowhere because some company had shared their contact information. Quickly she sorted the junk to the back to be tossed in the garbage as soon as she got to the house.

A voice called from the other side of the cluster, "You, too, huh?"

Anne smiled in recognition. "Betty, I don't know how this happens. It seems like every time I turn around I've gotten another home decor magazine. I only ordered one thing from a totally different magazine two years ago!"

Betty Graves came around the corner with an armful of mail hitched on her hip like a child. She shook her head. "Guess I should have stopped the mail while we were in Seaside, but I honestly didn't think we would be gone that long."

"How was the beach?" Anne asked, a hint of longing tingeing her words. It had been years since she had been to Florida.

The older woman wiped her glistening brow and said, "Lovely as always and, as always, too short a stay, even though we were there two weeks."

Betty lived further down the street in the neighborhood, but they frequently met at the mailboxes, and they enjoyed talking when they saw each other at the country club, where they were both members. Betty and her husband, Jim, had owned a beach house in Seaside since the late 1980s, when the town was just being developed. It was an easy walk to the beach, and Betty loved sitting on her upstairs porch at night, listening to the waves.

She looked at the stack in front of her and shook her head. "It's a good thing I remembered to put a stop on the mail when we leave next month."

"Oh?" Anne asked. "Where are you and Jim off to now?"

"Japan. He has to go somewhere over there for business and wanted me to go along. It's not that I mind the travel, but it would be nice to stay in one place for longer than a month."

Anne chuckled. She spent hours a day in the car, driving from doctors' offices to clinics, and sometimes even hospitals. She could well imagine putting that on a larger scale. Finished sorting the mail, she turned to head back to her car.

From behind her, she heard Betty call, "Oh, Anne! I meant to give you something."

Curious, Anne turned and saw Betty plop her stack of mail on the passenger seat of her car and return with a piece of paper.

"What's that?"

Betty glanced at it before handing it to Anne. "The Courtyard Chapel is just down the road from our house, and when we're there on Sundays, we walk to church and sit outside for the worship service. Well, when we were there last week, the pastor's wife was handing out flyers for a retreat they're holding next month."

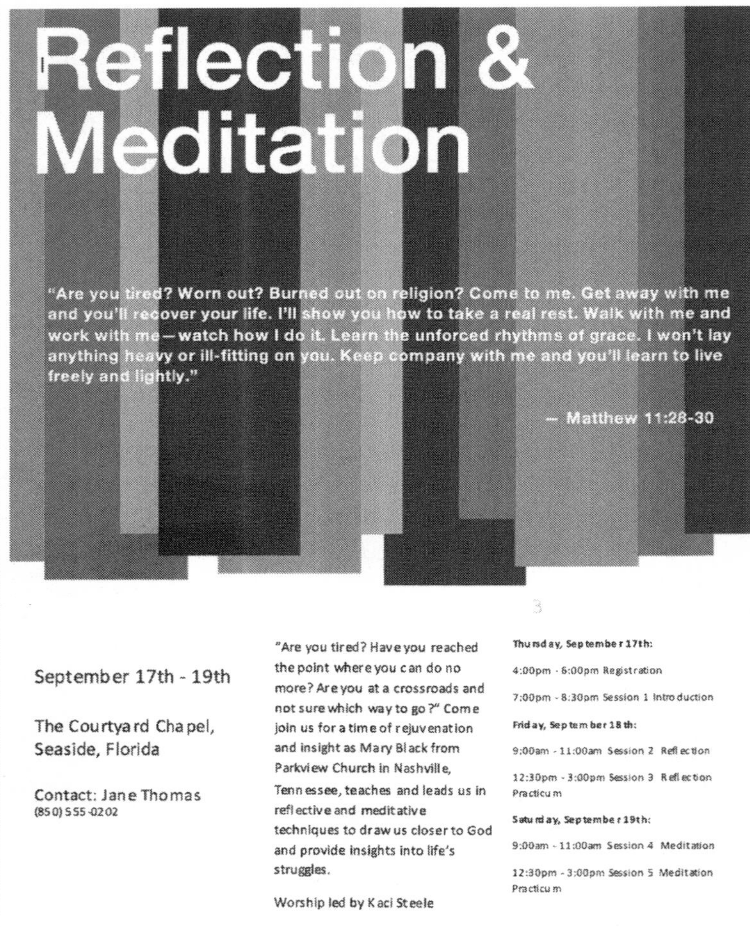

Anne felt something in her spirit stir as she began to read the flyer. The gentle tugging turned insistent, much like her son Theo's grip on her hand when he was ready to leave a store and she was still browsing. It was the same weekend that her women's group held their retreat. She looked up at Betty and found the older woman watching her. "Wow," Anne said.

Betty grinned. "I know. Sounds great, right? If I were sure we would be back from Japan by then, I would go. As a matter of fact, I brought the flyer home to check it against our travel dates, but I just can't make it work. I figured you or someone at your church might be interested."

Anne didn't reply but knew she could think of at least three other women who would fit that bill. Betty continued, "And if you do decide to go, let me know. You and your guests are welcome to use our beach house."

"Betty! That's too much," Anne said, surprised by the generosity.

Betty waved off her protestation. "It's just going to sit empty, and Jim and I built it to be used. I can't think of any better purpose for it than as a haven for a church retreat." She turned to climb into her car and said, "Just shoot me a text, and let me know. I'll give you the address and key code."

Dumbfounded, Anne nodded, then slowly made her way to her own vehicle.

Chapter 2

Two days later, Lindsay opened the back door of her white Volvo SUV and her two towheaded girls tumbled out. She had parked in her usual spot on the second row of parking at Three Crosses Church. Off Highway 181, it was about twenty minutes from their home in Montrose, but the worship and teaching were well worth the drive.

Lindsay fondly twisted a finger-curled ringlet on each of the girls' heads then brushed a couple of wrinkles out of their matching dresses. Lindsay was glad they were of an age where she could still get away with dressing them alike, and she knew it would be sooner than she would like when one or the other would put her foot down. For now though, they were the picture-perfect family. Well, perfect minus one that Sunday.

Her husband, John, was a military contractor and traveled one weekend a month. Since it was that weekend, Lindsay decided to volunteer in the Sunday school classroom of Ellery, her youngest, in lieu of attending the service. She would miss the worship, one of her favorite parts of the service, but it always felt odd worshipping without John after nearly eleven years of marriage.

"Okay, loves, let's get you to your classrooms," she said as she tapped the comfort access button on the driver's door handle then took each girl by the hand and started off across the parking lot.

Her oldest, Abigail, waved happily to a child walking in with her parents. "There's Erica!" Each seven years old and only a week apart in birthdays, the two girls had become instant friends when Erica's family moved to Fairhope the previous year. Lindsay was grateful for their bond, having never formed any of her own since her family had moved so frequently when she was a child. Her father had been a chemical engineer with a national company that sent him all over the United States for consulting; they relocated him six times before she was fifteen. Thankfully, John was able to maintain a home base in Fairhope for as long as he wanted, given its proximity to Pensacola's Naval Air Station and his willingness to sacrifice one weekend a month.

Fairhope's location and small-town, homey feel had been the two biggest factors in their own move when she was pregnant with Abigail. Neither had wanted to raise a family in Montgomery, given its size and crime rate. As a state's attorney, Lindsay had seen more than her share of the criminal element as it passed through the halls of justice, and she readily had left it behind in favor of full-time motherhood.

Almost eight years and two kids later, though, Lindsay was beginning to wonder if she had made the right decision. Fairhope was the childhood she wanted for her daughters, but was it the adulthood she wanted for herself? She looked longingly at the church's prayer garden, a lovely pond offset by three pergolas and shaded by crape myrtle and birch trees. She knew she could really use some time over there just to sit and seek, but Abigail's gentle tug at her hand reminded her it wouldn't be that day.

Jess and Mitch sat near the end of their usual row in the middle of the church. She scanned the bulletin announcements and was unsurprised to see not only Muriel's name under the list of prayer requests but also that the women's retreat next month had been canceled. She had doubted anyone would want to take up the reins in Muriel's stead. Even though there were less than three weeks to go, there would be plenty of last-minute issues to tackle, the largest of which would be finding a speaker to take Muriel's place.

She glanced over at Mitch, who was glued to his smartphone, checking the rankings and prognostications on the bowl pairings. Jess jostled his elbow and showed him the bulletin. "Hey, the men's Bible study will be starting up soon. It'll be at seven thirty Wednesday mornings."

Mitch didn't look away from the phone's screen as he replied, "I have a weekly contractor meeting at that time."

Jess nodded, put the bulletin to the side, and waved at Anne as she walked into the sanctuary. With a smile of welcome, she picked up the pair of bulletins holding Anne's and Ted's seats. "So, I just saw that the retreat is officially canceled," Jess said as Anne settled herself in her seat.

Anne nodded. "I figured as much, but there is a possible alternative." She pulled a piece of paper out of her purse and handed it to Jess. "My neighbor down the street, Betty, just got back from her house in Seaside and said the Courtyard Chapel is hosting their first retreat the same weekend ours was scheduled."

Jess read over it and was caught by the verse from The Message version of Matthew. It seemed to glow on the page. Before she could comment, Ted slid into his seat next to Anne, children's church pager in hand, and the band began to play. The congregation rose to sing along. A few people, Ted and Anne included, raised their hands in worship, but to her left, Mitch stood stock still and silent.

He had been like that from the first time he agreed to attend church with Jess about six months into their relationship. She knew he didn't read the Bible that was stuck between his well-worn copies of *Fundamentals of Building Construction* and *The Complete History of Crimson Tide Football.* Equally concerning were his responses to attending any group outside the regular service, which were much the same as his earlier one: he had conflicting appointments that took precedence.

Yet there was another side to him. His care and consideration. His humor and love of history. His desire for a family and to remain in the area. If it weren't for the marriages of Anne and Ted and Lindsay and John, Jess would have jumped at any mention of a marriage proposal from Mitch. However, seeing how God was present in those two couples as they worshipped and lived had given Jess a new perspective on how a godly marriage should look, and she had a sinking feeling that a marriage with Mitch would be sorely lacking.

She glanced down at the flyer in her seat and decided a little relaxation and meditation might be just what she needed. If nothing else, she could use some insight into her struggle, and perhaps a different physical perspective would help with her current spiritual one.

"As long as Mitch is okay with it, I'm in," she said to Anne. She leaned forward to pull her phone out of her purse, but was stalled by the lead guitarist asking the congregation to stand for worship. She leaned over and whispered, "I'll text Deli right after church."

~~*

Delia "Deli" Preston hummed along to the latest Christian radio releases and absently ran her fingers through her longer-than-usual now-ebony hair as she drove down I-10 on her way back to Fairhope from New Orleans. It would be good to get home. While experiencing the latest addition to Haven's fleet of ginormous cruise ships had allowed her the opportunity to breathe some sea air, the sheer number of passengers, even on that maiden voyage, was fatiguing. She chuckled as she read the mile marker sign: eighty miles to home. It was almost comical for her to think of Fairhope, Alabama, as home after she had spent most of her nomadic life traipsing all over the Western Hemisphere, covering stories for various magazines and newspapers. Yet, it was.

She had arrived there in March three years prior, laptop and notepad in hand, ready to profile the annual arts and crafts festival for a Southern magazine, and had unexpectedly fallen in love with the city. Perhaps it was the odd amalgam of business, rural, and suburban peppered by low-hung live oaks that lined the road on the outskirts of town that called to her soul. Even though the quaint, Southern comfort found in a town just a hair over sixteen thousand souls should have been stifling to a woman who had happily shut the door on her unhappy small-town upbringing, it was just the opposite. Sunburnt by bright lights and busier cities, the warmth and charm that greeted her as she drove past the camellia-engulfed welcome sign at the turnoff for Scenic 98 had tugged awake an emotion she had thought long dead: contentment. During that entire assignment, she'd had to pinch herself back to the reality that awaited her in Atlanta.

A buzz from the passenger seat caught her ear. Some days she would like to chuck her phone out the window and forget it was ever an appendage that she couldn't remove. A quick glance at the screen revealed that it wasn't her agent or even the magazine editor berating her for the evaporating print deadline.

Instead it was Jess. It wasn't uncommon for the two of them to text various insights or prayer requests, but Jess knew Deli would be traveling and normally didn't reach out unless it was something important. Concerned it might be a status change for the worse for Muriel, Deli glanced at the clock on the dashboard and her fuel gauge, now about a quarter tank, and decided the next Biloxi exit would be her best bet. She pulled into the truck stop, turned off the car, then reached for the phone. One thumbprint later, and the text appeared.

Deli heaved a sigh of relief. Then her brow furrowed as she leafed through her mental calendar. She didn't use the one on her phone, preferring instead to maintain the keen memorizing skills she had picked up in journalism school. September 17 through 19. By then the current article would be submitted and edited, ready for press. The Christmas profiles of the South's mansions she was contracted to complete for her freelance job wouldn't need prep time until mid-October. This could work. As a bonus, it would be nice to go someplace and leave her travel writer hat at home. With a quick smile, she dashed off her reply.

~~*

Jess slipped her phone back into her purse and smiled at Anne. "Deli's in!"

Anne grinned. "Great! That just leaves Lindsay. I'll take her out for coffee tomorrow when the kids are in school. She needs a getaway as much as the rest of us."

Jess nodded, but looked doubtful. Lindsay, with her brilliant but overly analytical mind, would likely come up with a number of reasons why she couldn't, even though in her heart she would know she should.

Seeing Mitch coming out of the men's room, Jess reached over and hugged Anne briefly. "Gotta go. You know Mitch doesn't like to wait with the church lunch crowd." She hurried after her boyfriend, who had already reached the exit. Jess turned as she realized she still held the flyer. "Mind if I keep this? Might need the ammunition!" she said with a wry grin and a wave good-bye.

Anne shook her head and called, "I'll get it from you tomorrow. I have to stop by the hospital in the morning anyway."

~~*

The door closed behind Jess, leaving Anne alone in the front of the church. Her smile of sympathy at Jess's impending discussion with Mitch brightened to delight as she spotted her son racing toward her from the children's church. Seeing her sullen daughter reluctantly bringing up the rear behind her father, Anne forced her rapidly depleting joy into high gear. "Hi, guys! How was church?" The youth were encouraged to worship in their own service, which was held during the main worship time. It was usually packed with kids from the middle and high school classes and led by the youth leaders and a student worship band.

Kelsie mumbled an answer under her breath that Anne decided was something along the lines of "fine." Theo thrust his worksheet about the five loaves and two fish into her hand and began happily chattering about the story.

Anne listened halfheartedly, her attention focused on her ginger-headed daughter. All reports from the youth pastors indicated that Kelsie participated and seemed to enjoy worshipping with her peers, but every Sunday since the start of school, Anne had seen only an increasingly irritable thirteen-year-old going to and coming from the service. She sighed and caught her husband's eye. With a shrug and a helpless shake of his head, Ted scooped up Theo in his arms and threw him over his shoulder. The little boy squealed with delight, eliciting the tiniest upward turn of his sister's lips.

Anne worried about her daughter diving headlong from the usual teenage angst into full-on depression. She also worried that Kelsie would, in an effort to distinguish herself and her growing need for independence, fall into the wrong crowd at the public middle school she attended. There were so many problems in the world, and the culture had turned morality on its head, calling wrong right and right wrong. It definitely wasn't the world she had grown up in. But then her mother had worried about her as well, and Anne figured she had turned out all right: happily married with two healthy children and a successful career as a drug rep for a major pharmaceutical company.

Taking another surreptitious glance at Kelsie, whose sequined Chuck Taylors were infinitely more interesting than her surroundings, Anne sighed again. She realized this wasn't the place to press the issue of Kelsie's mood. Instead she ran her hand over Theo's head after Ted returned him to the floor and said, "Let's head home now that everyone's here. The Crock-Pot should be filled with a nice, bubbly lasagna!" Theo's cheers for his favorite pasta dish followed her as she turned to lead the family out to the parking lot.

After their food orders were placed, Jess waited for a commercial break on the game to broach the subject of the retreat with Mitch, a difficult endeavor given the number of TV screens in the restaurant. She figured if he went to church for her, the least she could do was go to McHenry's, his favorite sports bar, for lunch afterward. That was what good couples did, wasn't it? Compromise?

Finally, his attention drifted from the TVs to look around the room. "Not as full today," he said. "A lot of people must have traveled to the Alabama game."

She took a quick breath and laid the flyer on the table. "One of Anne's friends is just back from her house in Seaside and brought this with her."

Mitch smiled indulgently and skimmed the paper. "Sounds like something up your alley." He read the dates again, and his gaze turned speculative, then disappointed. "That's the weekend of the big game against LSU. I just got us tickets yesterday."

"Oh, I didn't know." She paused. Even though she had graduated from Auburn, she had never developed an appreciation for football. Whenever they went to a game, she would sit and people-watch while Mitch whooped and hollered at every touchdown and bad call. A wisp of an idea flitted through her head. "Why don't you take Guy with you instead? I'm sure you'll have friends on both sides there. You could set up a tailgate and make a full day of it."

Mitch looked intrigued. "That's a good idea," he mused as he pulled out his phone to check the calendar. "Since you won't be here for church, I don't have to go, and we could overnight up there and drive back Sunday. Make a full weekend of it. That's a great idea, honey!" He blew her a kiss as his eyes were drawn back to the game.

Jess slipped the flyer back into her purse and swallowed the emotional lead sinker that had robbed her of a reply. If it was such a great idea, why did she feel worse now than before she brought it up?

~~*

Lunch finished and the table cleared by a reluctant Kelsie, Anne and Ted stood side by side at the sink, Anne rinsing and Ted putting the dishes in the dishwasher. Through the French doors at the back of the condo, they could easily see Theo kicking around a soccer ball. In the air was the muffled beat of Kelsie's iPod churning out the latest from Selena Gomez and Taylor Swift.

Anne could feel Ted's surreptitious glances every time she handed him a plate. The man had always been able to read her moods, even in high school. She knew he wanted to ask, yet she had no words to explain her roiling conglomeration of emotions. She sighed as the volume ratcheted up to blaring when the playlist reached Kelsie's favorite songs. Defeat and dejection slumped Anne's shoulders. She shook the water from her hands, and patted them with a nearby kitchen towel. "I'll go tell her to turn it down."

Before she could turn to go, Ted grabbed her still-moist hand and pulled her into a hug. "Give it a minute, hon."

Anne melted into his embrace, exhausted by what was becoming a never-ending battle with her daughter. "What happened to our sweet, funny little girl?" she mumbled into his shoulder, on the verge of tears. "She doesn't say two words to me anymore, and there was a time not that long ago when we couldn't run out of things to talk about."

Anne felt Ted's soothing hand as it skimmed down her back. He didn't say a word, and for that she was grateful. She knew he had learned the hard way years ago the difference between the times when she needed him to fix something and those when she merely needed to vent her frustrations.

The song ended, and the volume decreased noticeably. Still, Anne stood wrapped in Ted's arms, soaking up his silent support. At length she turned her head to rest her cheek on his shoulder, snuggling in a bit closer. Ted squeezed her then returned to his soothing caress.

"Is it time to look at sending her to counseling?" Anne asked. "The last thing I want is for her to feel like there's something wrong with her, but what if there really is something wrong? I would hate myself if we didn't get her help when she needed it."

Ted tucked his cheek against the top of her head. "What if you two just need a break from each other? You know, this retreat will give both of you some breathing room, and maybe it'll put some things into perspective."

"Hmmm," she replied. "Hadn't thought of it that way. I was just looking for something to do since our retreat was canceled, and I had the time already blocked out." She paused and reviewed what she'd said. "Well, that and—I can't really explain it—but when Betty showed me the flyer, something tugged at me, and I knew I needed to go."

Ted smiled and squeezed her again. "Well, there's your answer. Sometimes the Holy Spirit gently tugs, and sometimes He speaks, but we've got to listen and follow, no matter the method."

Anne chuckled in agreement as the iPod once again gained volume. "I'll go tell Kelsie that I'll be gone for a few days then. And I'll try to get her to turn down the music."

Anne tapped on the door to her daughter's room. The "no entry" sign that she usually hung on the door handle when she was doing her homework or just wanted some privacy from Theo was not posted. Anne knew the girl couldn't hear the knock, so she turned the handle and peeked around the door. Kelsie lay prone on her bed, legs crossed at the ankles, casually tapping the air to the beat of "the Bieb's" latest hit. Her eyes were glued to the magazine in front of her. Anne cleared her throat and said, "Kelsie? Sweetie, can we talk?"

Gaze still riveted by the article, Kelsie shrugged and replied, "I guess."

Ignoring the girl's lack of enthusiasm, Anne settled on the corner of the bed. "Honey, I'm worried about you. Are you okay?" Kelsie didn't reply and instead simply turned a page of the magazine. "You never invite your friends over anymore. I remember we would have so much fun with movie and popcorn nights. Then y'all would have a dance party, and your dad and I would be the audience. Wouldn't you like to do that again?"

Kelsie shrugged. Anne waited, and just when it seemed that was all the answer she was going to get, Kelsie added, "I don't know, maybe."

Anne smiled brightly. At least that was two more words than Kelsie usually used around her. "Well, think about it, but that wasn't the reason I came up here."

Kelsie heaved a sigh and then broke her record on sentence length: "I know. You want me to turn the music down."

Anne bit back a sharp retort, reminding herself that at least Kelsie was speaking in longer sentences. "Well, there is that, but also I wanted to tell you that I'm going to go out of town for a couple of days in a few weeks."

Kelsie perked up at the news. "Where? When?" She was back to single words.

Anne decided to take it as a win since Kelsie was at least showing interest in something beyond her magazine and music. "I'm going to a church retreat with some of my friends in Seaside, Florida. It's the second weekend in September. Your dad will take you to church on Sunday, and I'll leave some casseroles for dinner."

Anne watched Kelsie absorb the details. *The child might make a great poker player in the future,* she thought wryly. Then she asked, "What are you thinking?"

Kelsie shrugged and went back to her magazine. "Have fun."

Jess pulled her car into the drive of her Arts and Crafts bungalow in the Fruits and Nuts district of Fairhope. Mitch got out and headed to the front yard to fetch the Sunday paper that had landed just inside the wrought-iron fence that encompassed her yard. Her mother had moved to the cottage in the early nineties after she and Jess's father divorced. For most of high school, Jess was shuttled between there and Mobile, as joint custody had been the judge's decision when neither parent would allow sole custody, even with regular visitation.

Jess opened the back door, tossed her keys and purse on the counter, and glanced around the kitchen. As a teenager, she had hated the house and everything it represented: a broken family, a failed marriage, and continued animosity. When her mother had called her that fateful day with her diagnosis of stage four pancreatic cancer, Jess had pushed all that aside, left her position at the hospital in Auburn, and returned.

Sometime between moving back into her old bedroom and moving her mom permanently into the cancer ward of The Hospital at Fairhope Jess's anger had cooled and her broken heart had mended.

Now the house was merely a house. As Jenna's only child, Jess had inherited it at her mother's passing. Rather than selling it and returning to Auburn as she had originally thought, she found herself happy to remain and was hired at the hospital, which was only a stone's throw away.

Mitch came in the front door and settled himself on the couch with the paper for their customary Sunday afternoon together while she went back to her room to change into more comfortable clothes. After a few minutes, he called, "Hey, babe, did you see that the house just down the street sold? I heard the new owners were planning to tear it down and build something bigger."

Donning an old Auburn T-shirt, Jess replied, "You mean the Andersons'? No, I hadn't heard that. Do you know if they've found a builder?"

Mitch owned a private contracting firm and had built several new homes in the Daphne/Fairhope area over the years. Business was booming as each little town was experiencing growth spurts. Jess could hear the paper rustling as he turned the pages. "No, but I'm going to ask around—maybe drop by the listing agent's office and leave a business card that could be passed along at closing."

Jess reappeared in the living room. With her shoulder-length blonde hair tied back in a ponytail, a faded T-shirt, jeans, and sneakers, she looked ten years younger. "Want something to drink?" she asked as she pulled open the fridge door.

He glanced over and smiled, the appreciation of her relaxed state glowing in his eyes. He had said on more than one occasion that he enjoyed seeing her in casual clothes. He couldn't care less if she wore makeup, saying she was prettier to him without it. "Anything's good."

She smiled back and pulled out a Miller Lite for him and a lime La Croix water for herself, popped the tops of each, and settled next to him. Mitch raised his arm so she could tuck her head against his shoulder and pick out her own articles of interest on the page. He brushed a kiss across the top of her head and returned to his reading.

Jess loved Sunday afternoons. The struggle between football and faith took a time-out, and she felt the peace Muriel had mentioned. They read the paper, traded stories from their week, and often watched a movie snuggled on the couch, simply enjoying each other's company. These were the hours that could lull her into forgetting her concerns about their unequal faiths and tempt her to accept his unspoken proposal. At the heart of it all, he was a good and caring man. She leaned up and kissed his stubbly cheek.

Mitch glanced away from the paper to smile at her, a question in his eyes. She shook her head, her cheek rubbing against the fine cotton of his dress shirt, and answered, "Just glad to be here with you." He squeezed her in reply as they returned to their reading.

Chapter 3

Whole Latte Caffeine was the town's oldest and, in Lindsay's opinion, best coffee shop. It didn't hurt that it was located conveniently two doors down from the dance studio where her daughters spent a few hours every week. Sharing the same roof with the three-generation-run bookstore, they had recently expanded, adding a wine bar in the back. At night, students from the university a block over would crowd the back room, but during the day it was the front that held the most occupants.

Lindsay sat in one of the mismatched iron-backed chairs facing the corrugated metal surrounding the counter and watched the other patrons. Snippets of their conversations were punctuated by the whir of the espresso machine and the intermittent calling of names, heralding the completion of some caffeinated concoction. When Anne had called on Sunday, asking to meet that morning after the kids were in school, Lindsay had welcomed the distraction from the piles of laundry and stacks of dishes that sat awaiting her attention.

What happened to my life? she thought as she watched the busy professionals clad in their work uniforms of skirts and button-down shirts, jackets, and ties. She had once been a member of that club, brokering deals and writing contracts. Lindsay took a sip of her green tea and looked down at her yoga pants and cover-up, the uniform of the stay-at-home mom. Granted it was much more physically comfortable than the Ann Taylor suit the lady currently placing her order wore, but emotionally? That was a different story.

She jumped a bit and looked up as a hand squeezed her shoulder. With a smile, she reached up and squeezed back as Anne plopped her purse on the table, shaking Lindsay's tea mug. "Sorry I'm late," she said as she ran a hand through her auburn bangs to move them out of her eyes. "Got caught up at one of the offices, restocking samples."

Anne, a successful pharmaceutical rep with two kids, had returned to the workforce right after each child was born and had never looked back. While her husband was an ophthalmologist and made a good salary, they had just graduated from LSU when they married and had Kelsie a year later. She hadn't had the same opportunity as Lindsay to have her career before children, which made Lindsay wonder if that was the better choice. Would she not feel so guilty about leaving her children to return to work if she hadn't had the time to process the ins and outs, wherefores and whys?

"Lins?" Anne asked, her brow furrowed. "You okay?"

Lindsay jerked her thoughts back and smiled ruefully. "Yes, sorry. Just woolgathering."

"Well, let me get a drink, and maybe we can turn this into a knitting bee," Anne replied as she dug out her wallet and turned for the counter.

With a wry chuckle, Lindsay shook her head. That's what she loved about Anne. She was always ready to be an ear, a helper, and even a shoulder, whatever the situation warranted. A few minutes later, she returned to the table. "What did you get?" Lindsay asked, knowing her friend's penchant for lattes.

"I got that new spice latte they've added for fall. It sounded divine!"

Lindsay agreed, but on her latest round of healthy eating, dairy was second only to white carbs on the evil foods list. She waited until Anne was settled with her drink before diving in to the reason for the meeting. Ever the lawyer, she always functioned better with an agenda, even for social gatherings. "So, what's up?"

"Nothing much," Anne answered blithely. "I mainly just wanted to check in on you since we won't be having our weekly Bible study. How have you been?"

Certain Anne wouldn't let her get away with a blithe, "Fine," Lindsay sighed and admitted, "I'm struggling."

"Oh no! What's happened?"

"Nothing really. I mean, John is fine, as are the girls. Abigail likes her new teacher, and Ellery is excited to finally be in kindergarten and going to 'big girl school.'" She paused and looked away, blinking back the sudden welling of tears. Lindsay felt Anne's hand pat her forearm and welcomed the comfort. Drowning the lump in her throat with a swig of green tea that scalded her tongue, she grimaced then said, "John and I had always agreed that when we started our family, I would stay home. I really wanted that." Uncertain of how to put her roiling emotions into words, she paused.

"But?" Anne prompted.

Lindsay shook her head, then bit her lip before continuing. "God, I feel so guilty for saying this, but what about my life and my goals?" She stopped, unable to say more.

Anne took a sip of her latte, sympathy etched in her brow as she waited for her friend to find the words.

After a moment's contemplation, Lindsay continued. "I'm losing myself in Barbies and tea parties and 'Mommy, where are yous?' I love my girls and wouldn't trade the choices I've made to stay home with them, but somewhere along the way, I lost me." She shook her head, perplexed. "I was a litigator in front of the state supreme court!" Lindsay said, exasperation seeping into her words. "Now I mediate time-shares for TV and computer use and form arguments for why bedtime is at eight and not eight thirty."

Lindsay paused, feeling niggling pinpricks of guilt, then quietly admitted, "I know what I chose back then, but what if I don't want to stay at home now?" She took another much smaller sip of tea and added, "It's not about the income. We're fine on John's salary alone, although it would be nice to have a cushion, given the almost constant threat of military cutbacks."

Anne's sympathetic smile framed a question that made Lindsay shake her head in exasperation. "What does John think?"

"He's fine with whatever I decide," Lindsay answered, irritation lacing her tone, "which is very supportive, but not very helpful."

Anne shook her head, her confusion evident. "Not following you."

Lindsay sighed and toyed with a napkin. "He's so supportive either way that it makes me feel guiltier, oddly enough." She tore the edge of one piece and began absently folding it. "It would be nice if he would tell me what to do and give me a definitive answer: go back to work or stay home."

Anne's eyebrows lifted. "So you could blame him if it doesn't turn out like you planned?"

"Ouch." Lindsay grimaced, drawing her hands away from their idle work. "I hadn't thought of it that way." She ducked her head, then meekly asked, "Am I a horrible person?"

Anne laughed and shook her head. "No, just someone who doesn't have an answer and is looking everywhere for one."

"I've prayed and asked God for His will and purpose, but I don't have peace either way."

Anne took a sip of her latte and ventured, "It might help for you to get away for a bit. You know, take some time to weigh the pros and cons away from them so you can think clearly rather than through the guilt." She paused to fish the flyer out of her purse and hand it to Lindsay. "Betty brought this back from her trip to her beach house. It looks like a perfect way to recharge and think about things. Jess and Deli are going, and Betty said she was more than happy to let us use her house, which is just down the street from the church. Why don't you come with us to the retreat?"

Lindsay scanned the flyer, rapidly assimilating the information with her family's schedule, then shook her head. "I don't see how I can go. John's got a big meeting that next week, so he'll be preparing for it. What would I do with the girls?" She pushed it back toward Anne with a more decisive shake of her head and stirred her green tea.

Obviously not ready to concede defeat, Anne asked, "What about his parents? Won't they be back from their trip out west by then?" Lindsay's brow began to furrow as she absorbed the new detail, leading Anne to press, saying, "I'm sure they're missing the girls and would love to spend time with them."

Anne sensed that, while her resolve was weakening, Lindsay remained doubtful. "It's only for three days—the same amount of time we would have committed to our church retreat," she reminded. Then, putting on her best impression of a charmingly imploring Theo, she played her final card, "Ask them before you say no."

Lindsay couldn't help but smile as she rolled her eyes.

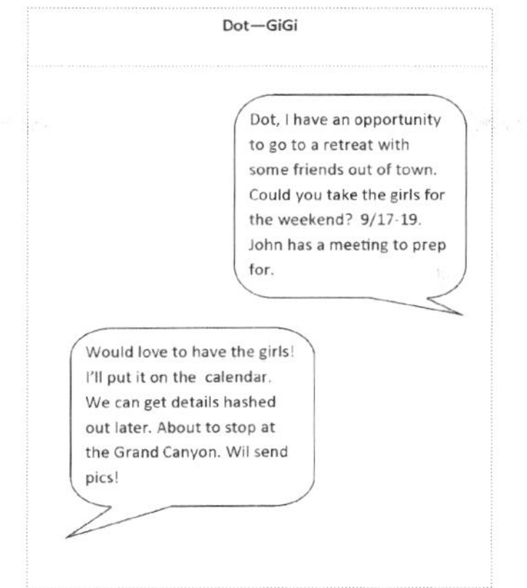

Lindsay smiled with reluctant acceptance. "Looks like I'm in. Dot is thrilled to take the girls, which would be great for John; he can have the house to himself to prep and relax."

Anne ignored her friend's less-than-enthusiastic response and replied, "Great! I'll call the church and Betty and let them know we'll be coming." She reached across the table and squeezed Lindsay's arm. "It'll do you good. You'll see."

Her girl time with Anne finished, and it being too early to pick up the girls from school, Lindsay headed to the one place she'd longed to be on Sunday. Seated in the church's prayer garden, she gazed over the shrubs that surrounded the pergola and into the quiet pond. The stillness was punctuated by the hum of an occasional car on the highway and the drone of a tractor engine as it brought hay to the cows in the field next door. Fairhope was so different from the rapid, albeit still Southern, pace of Montgomery. There was a peace there that she had never found in the state capital.

"Why is this decision so hard, Lord? Why is it more than a simple yes or no?" she asked, pain leaching into her voice. "Does it all come down to a matter of pride and saving face against the coworkers who told me I was too type-A to last as a stay-at-home mom? Am I being selfish for putting my wants and what I feel I need above the life I had planned for my girls?" She paused, working up her courage to give voice to her greatest guilt-ridden thought. Even then it came out only as whisper: "Was Daddy right all along when he said I couldn't stick to anything?"

There were no answers in the wind or in her spirit, and Lindsay wept the bitter tears of guilt and shame.

~~*

Deli closed the lid of the washing machine on the first load of laundry she had from her trip. Of all the inconveniences of travel, not being able to launder her clothes ranked right up there with airport delays. Thankfully, she had been in the Caribbean rather than the mountains, and her wardrobe of shorts, blouses, and swimsuits would be refreshed quickly. Laundry was not one of her favorite chores.

The water rushed into the drum muffling the ding of the microwave, but Deli was already headed back that way, ready for the Lean Cuisine she had just nuked. With her travel schedule so intermittent, she had found cooking for herself wasteful. The leftovers often sat for several days in their Tupperware dishes, making her refrigerator more a laboratory than an appliance.

She poured the meal out onto a plate, grabbed a glass of tea, and headed over to the table. Not one for watching much TV, she flipped on the surround sound, her one splurge when she bought the house. One benefit that actually came with it though was the close proximity of the Fairhope Pier. When the realtor had mentioned it, Deli had nodded but focused on the house itself.

The pier turned out to be a pleasant surprise and one that she found herself using more often than not when she was home. It was a beautiful place for a run. She ran from her house downtown, down the hill at the park, and out to the pier at least three times a week. The runs were as much for relaxation as exercise, although she was highly aware of the need for cardio to maintain her weight. Cruise line and airport food were not good for the waistline.

Though eager to stretch her legs, she slid the run a notch down on her mental to-do list. First and foremost, she needed to finish her write-up on the *Silver Queen*, but that really wouldn't be a chore. The ship was beautiful and jam-packed with every activity one would want to fill the hours of the "at sea" days. After giving her food a quick stir, she flipped open her MacBook Pro and called up the article's file.

"Moby Deck's Silver Lining" by Delia Preston. Seeing her given name always took Deli slightly aback. She had been known as Deli for a good deal longer than Delia, having been tagged with the nickname back in grade school. She was overweight as a child, and her classmates' teasing escalated to outright bullying after the arrival of Jamie Rogers. That cute boy, whom she had admired when he moved into town, had turned ugly after learning of her crush, taunting that she was so fat she could eat an entire deli and still be hungry. After months of abuse at school and no support at home, Delia had disappeared, and Deli was born.

Quiet and shy, she had worked hard at blending in. Her average grades and low self-esteem coupled with the harassment drove Deli into books, where she discovered a love of the written word. In high school, she signed up for every English and journalism class she could, and excelled in them all. She dreamed of leaving Mapdot, Arkansas, for Chicago and the *Tribune*. A scholarship to Northwestern sealed the deal, and it wasn't long before she closed the door on every part of the past, except the name. She just couldn't shake it. As a freshman, she tried using Delia, but whenever a teacher called on her as Delia, she didn't recognize it as her name.

Her first-year roommate, who was a psych major, identified some of the behavioral signs that Deli had been bullied as a child. Jennifer had encouraged her to take advantage of the free counseling offered by the department's clinic. She was also the first person to talk to her about Jesus. Deli's parents had been dragged to church on Christmas and Easter by their parents, so they were less than interested in raising their daughter in any sort of faith.

But when Jennifer talked about her faith, Deli had begun to wonder if there was something more to it than a baby and a guy who was tortured to death. She had asked her graduate counselor in one of their sessions and was encouraged by her to explore Christianity and visit a few of the area churches.

Jennifer had gladly taken Deli with her to her church, a large nondenominational one on the outskirts of Chicago, and patiently answered all of her questions. It was Jennifer who had led her through the sinner's prayer while sitting on Deli's bed in their dorm room.

Between learning about her newfound identity in God and the formal counseling, Deli's emotional abuse healed. On the heels of that freedom came the desire to lose the weight she now knew was a shield that she had hidden behind. So she added a variety of physical education classes to her electives, and the weight began to fall off. Finally free of the past, she kept the nickname as a reminder of her healing. It was a battle scar of sorts.

Jennifer now had a thriving faith-based therapy practice in Vernon Hills, and they spoke on the phone about every six months or so. More frequently were the e-mail forwards of various devotionals and articles of interest.

A banner popped up on the laptop's screen, and Deli decided Jennifer's ears must have been burning. She clicked on the notice to open the e-mail bearing Jennifer's name. Giving the devotional a quick skim, she flagged it to read later when she had time to focus on it more fully, and turned back to the article she was writing. She absently spooned a bite of the Lean Cuisine meal into her mouth and got to typing.

~~*

Anne pulled into the parking lot at Dr. Rucker's office and squeezed into a spot between two larger SUVs. In the back seat sat bags of take-out from a funky little bistro downtown. Her company had sent out the updates on the new line of medicines that had been approved, and she would be presenting while the staff would be munching.

She glanced at the clock and saw she was a bit early, so she decided to make good on her promise to call to register for the retreat. Pulling out her phone and the flyer, she dialed and waited. After three rings, the line was answered. Anne introduced herself and the reason for the call, asking if it was too late to be added to the roster. The question was greeted with an enthusiastic response.

"Oh heavens no!" Jane replied, her genial tone warming the airwaves. "We have plenty of room. We had been planning to have a small group of locals this first year to try it out, but it's already grown beyond what I expected. Y'all are more than welcome to come!"

"The flyer didn't mention a registration fee. Will there be materials to purchase?"

"I knew we had left something off!" Jane laughed. "Yes, you'll get a name tag and binder with the speaker's notes and exercises. Have you ever heard Mary Black speak?" Before Anne could say yea or nay, Jane rambled on, "She's absolutely wonderful! She attends church here when she's in the area, and over the last couple of years, I've gotten to know her well. I had no idea when she first started coming that she was such a gifted speaker, but what can I say? You never know a person until you take the time to ask questions!"

That settled, Anne gave the names of the other women. After hanging up, she sat for a moment and looked at the phone. As much as she hated that Muriel was hurting, this felt right. God was definitely up to something.

Chapter 4

Seaside

Jane Thomas hung up the phone and walked through the kitchen of her Seagrove Beach cottage to the living room. "Well, that makes thirty!" she announced brightly to her husband, the Courtyard Chapel's pastor, who sat on the couch with their granddaughter. With the football game muted on the TV across the room, his attention was focused on bouncing the two-year-old on his lap.

"That's great news, Jane!" Greg exclaimed. "This was a good idea, wasn't it, Rebecca?" he asked the giggling little girl. "Grandpa might need to look into something for the men at some point." He paused in his bouncing, suddenly deep in thought. "Or maybe a couples' retreat would be a better place to start. Women will typically drag their husbands whereas men often won't go on their own."

Jane smiled at the pair as Greg dreamed of future retreat topics. Settling her matronly frame in her armchair, she pulled out a legal pad to add the names she had written on a piece of scratch paper. "Most of them are locals, and there are a couple who own houses here that are coming back simply for the retreat. These four, though, have never been here! Betty Graves took the flyer with her back to Fairhope and told them about it."

Jane's sunny disposition made her a natural as a pastor's wife. Kind and caring, with a smile that warmed from the inside, she was always ready to see the brighter side of life. The retreat had been the suggestion of one of the other locals who regularly attended the chapel, and Jane had leaped on the idea. She hosted the women's Bible studies during the fall and spring, and this was the perfect next step.

She and Greg had been at the chapel for five years after retiring from pastoring at a megachurch in California. One of their daughters had settled there and had called them when she heard about an opening for a pastor. Previously the chapel had relied on itinerants or guest speakers, but a movement within the homeowners' association led to the establishment of a full-time position. It was just the lifestyle they were hoping to find before retiring altogether in ten years or so.

She read through the names on the list in her lap and closed her eyes, asking God to bless each lady with insight and wisdom. A giggle from her granddaughter opened her eyes, and Jane found Rebecca at her feet, untying her shoes. With a shake of her head, she leaned over and picked her up. "Oh no, pumpkin! Not my shoes again!"

A few days later and a few miles down the road in Seacrest, the crash of the Gulf's waves mingled with the plucks and strums of a classical guitar as Kaci Steele practiced the acoustic versions of the worship songs she would play at the Courtyard Chapel's women's retreat. Earthy, leaning toward boho-chic, the striking tomboy balanced the guitar on one knee and kept time with the other. Her long, thin fingers, turned steely from years of guitar and mandolin picking, gracefully moved over the neck, pressing and releasing strings as the chords on her sheet music directed. Her golden retriever, Blue, lay in the floor at her feet.

There was no room in the chapel's chancel for additional accompaniment of other musicians and instruments, and the atmosphere really didn't lend itself to any style of music other than acoustic. The mission-style church possessed soaring white tongue-in-groove ceilings with open beams accented by a rich heart pine floor. When Kaci had walked through the door on her first trip to the area some ten years ago, her jaw had dropped in awe at the quiet simplicity and the hushed presence that permeated the air inside.

She finished the last chord and held the note as the strings faded, her husky alto voice a perfect match for the twang of the guitar. When the music died, she looked down at Blue and asked, "What do you think, buddy? Think it'll pass muster?" Blue perked his ears up at the question, then thumped his thick, shaggy tail against the hardwood floor in agreement.

Kaci leaned down and scratched him between his ears in thanks. She lifted the guitar off her lap and placed it back in its case. She would love to have a display area in the carriage house for her beautiful instruments, but that would mean risking untangling Blue's fine hair from the strings. As it was, the sunlight that streamed through the sliding glass doors that led to the balcony lit up every hairball on the pine floors. With a fond shake of her head at the sight, she patted him on his side and made a mental note to call the housekeeper to come sometime that week.

With the final head count for the retreat at thirty, Mary Black had her work cut out for her. She had already planned the verse and word study for the reflection portion of the teaching, but now she had the meditation portion to complete. This wasn't her usual route for teaching meditation on the Word, but time was short, and so she would have to condense. Although she always relied on the Holy Spirit's direction for her notes, she needed to be doubly sensitive so as not to emphasize the wrong aspect or underemphasize one that would be pivotal.

At her request, Jane had e-mailed the list of the attendees so that Mary could pray over them and allow the Holy Spirit to direct her to the verses that would be the most beneficial. She wasn't prophetic enough to match specific names to specific verses, but she could be sensitive in the selection and trust Him to put the right one in the right hand. So, now as she sat on the balcony of her condo overlooking the park and within view of the chapel, Bible open and laptop at the ready, she prayed for wisdom and insight, then turned the page.

Chapter 5

The Road in Between

"Okay, loves," Lindsay said, glancing in the rear-view mirror at the two girls in the back seat. They had just arrived at the school and pulled into the drop-off line. "Daddy will pick you up from school today and take you to dance class." Seeing the disappointment in their eyes, she offered, "If you're very good, he may take to you to the bookstore to pick out a book on the way home." Abigail cheered at the thought and began unbuckling her booster seat, as Lindsay pulled closer to the front of the line.

Ellery, though, remained pensive. "Mommy, don't go," came the soft plea from the back seat. Lindsay's heart melted. She swallowed the guilt and pulled to a stop. Sliding out of the driver's side, she opened the door to the back seat and found her, lower lip trembling and on the verge of tears. Though Lindsay and John had taken a couple of "Mommy and Daddy only" trips before, and his parents had watched the girls, Ellery had been two at the time. She likely had no memory of those getaways.

Abigail happily climbed out of the car and waved through the open door. "'Bye, Mommy! Love you!"

"Love you, too, sweet pea! Have a great day at school!" Lindsay smiled and blew her a kiss, then she returned her attention to her youngest. She leaned in and kissed the little girl's soft cheek, breathing in the lingering scent of baby on her rapidly growing child. "Sweetie, I know you don't want me to go, but if I don't, Gigi and Pop will be so sad. They are so excited about your staying at their house."

Apparently Ellery had forgotten that little detail, and she brightened considerably at the words. "I'm staying with Gigi and Pop?"

Lindsay tweaked the girl's nose. "Yes, you are, you goose! And I'm sure they brought you something neat from their trip."

Seemingly mollified by the new information, Ellery sat still as Lindsay unbuckled her car seat and pulled her backpack off the floorboard. Lindsay stepped back to allow her to climb down from the SUV then offered her the backpack. Ellery smiled and wrapped herself around her mother's leg. Giving it a tight squeeze, she said, "Have fun on your trip, Mommy! Love you!" then ran off to the school's front door.

Lindsay shook her head in amazement at the girl's resilience as she closed the doors and called, "Love you, too, baby." She climbed back into the Volvo and whispered, "Angels and archangels, fold your wings over and under and around my little girls and keep them safe." A slight tap of the horn on the car behind her jolted her out of her prayer, and with a friendly wave to the mom behind her, she pulled out of the line.

She and the other ladies had decided there was no reason to leave for Seaside first thing in the morning, so she had suggested to John that they have breakfast after she dropped off the little girls and before she had to pick up the big girls. Her bags were already packed and stowed in the trunk, and she was ready to set out at any time. John had happily agreed, suggesting Fairhope's oldest restaurant and his favorite place.

Five minutes later, she pulled into a spot in front of the diner, a few cars down from John's old Land Rover. It had been a combined college graduation and grad school acceptance gift, and he swore he would never sell it. Lindsay admitted there were quite a few memorable experiences tied to it, not the least how carefully he had detailed it to take her on their first date. She waved to him through the windshield as he stood outside building, waiting for her.

"Hey, babe," she said.

He grabbed her hand and opened the door to show her through. With a mischievous grin, he answered, "Long time no see!"

Lindsay teasingly jabbed her elbow in his side as she passed in front of him. As soon as the aromas hit her senses, her stomach growled. John wrapped an arm around her waist and, tugging her back against him, whispered, "Still hungry?" into her ear. A becoming pink stole over her cheeks at the reminder of the reason for her hunger. Their morning marital activities had been more intense and energetic than usual, given she would be gone for a few days.

"For food, you goof!" she whispered back with a flirtatious smile. Married eleven years, he still had the power to make her heart turn over. She knew she was blessed to be called his wife.

The waitress noticed them and nodded to a table across the way. "Make yourselves at home. I'll be over with a menu in a bit."

John pushed Lindsay toward the table, and she threw him a mock glare over her shoulder. "Hey," he decried innocently, "you're the hungry one!"

~~*

Lindsay checked the clock as she secured her seat belt. Ten o'clock. Perfect timing since they wanted to leave Fairhope by ten thirty. John leaned through the window to steal one last kiss and dropped a napkin covered in his handwriting in her lap. "Thought you might want the directions to Pensacola handy."

Warmed by his thoughtfulness and thankful for the note since she wasn't as familiar with the back route as he was, Lindsay trailed her fingers along his cheek. "I love you so much," she murmured.

The corners of John's eyes crinkled up as he answered with their oft-used reply, "Forever and ever, amen." He leaned in once more and tapped a kiss to her nose. "Now, go! I'm going to have two weekends in a row without you, so the sooner you leave the sooner you get back."

She laughed, knowing his meeting the next weekend had been moved to D.C., and there was always a night during the week when he was at the base well past ten. Lindsay rolled up the window and, with a final wave, backed out of the lot. While sitting at the stoplight, she dashed off a quick group text.

Group MMS

To: Deli, Jess, Anne

Deli, heading your way now. Jess, you're next and we'll get Anne on the way out of town

Deli Preston

Ready when you are!

Jess McAdams

See you soon!

Anne Greeley

Need to dash off an email to Kelsie's science teacher about her homework and leave her a note about her book report. Will be ready when you get here!

They had decided the night before for Deli and Jess to be picked up first since they were in town and Anne was on the way out. Lindsay pulled up outside Deli's bungalow, but before she could cut the engine, Deli was tapping on the rear window of the SUV. Lindsay pressed the button to open the trunk door. "You eager to get out of town?"

Deli grinned and shook her head as she tossed her well-traveled suitcase into the back beside Lindsay's matching carry-on and makeup bag. "No, just a by-product of the life of a travel writer. I'm always pretty much ready to go at a moment's notice."

Lindsay shook her head. "Lady, you would have made a good marine!"

"No way! I am not an early bird," Deli countered with a chuckle. "If I can get away with it, I prefer to lounge in bed when I wake up rather than be rousted out." She slammed the trunk door shut and snagged a seat in the back. A complaining squeak rent the air as she sat. With a furrowed brow, she fished out a toy from beneath her and held it up for Lindsay to see. "Is Ellery missing something?"

Lindsay rolled her eyes heavenward. "So that's where Mr. Bubbles went! I looked high and low for that thing all evening when I took out the car seats. It's one of the attachments that hangs off the side. Ellery's really too old for him now, but he's a comforting familiarity. Just stick Mr. Bubbles in the back seat pocket, and I'll reattach him when we get home."

Deli did as Lindsay requested then fastened her seatbelt as Lindsay put the SUV back in drive. A few minutes later, they were pulling up in front of Jess's house. Seeing she wasn't waiting on the porch, Deli pulled out her phone. "I'll text her and let her know we're here," she said. However, before she could type a word, the lady in question appeared on her front stoop, suitcase in hand.

She, too, stashed her bag and then popped into the back seat. Lindsay turned and looked at the two with bemusement. "You know, I did shower this morning, girls. You could sit up here."

Jess shook her head and replied, "No, thank you. Back seat drivers make me nuts, and since you and Anne know where we're going, it's best the two of you are up front."

Reminded of the directions that were still nestled in her lap, Lindsay picked up the napkin to read John's artful handwriting. "Head to the country club and pick up Highway 32, take it to 95 and turn right. When you get to 98, turn left. The NAS entrance will be on the right. Wave hello for me and follow 98 through Pensacola." Noticing there was more on the back, she flipped it over and found the heart he had drawn. She chuckled and caressed the drawing with her thumb before laying it in the cup holder for Anne.

Anne clicked the icon to send her e-mail to Kelsie's science teacher about the girl's homework. She hadn't understood the concept of homeostasis, and Anne had worked on it with her for two hours, finally ending up answering some of the questions for her just to be finished by bedtime. That done, she pulled out a stack of colorful notes to tag the various Tupperware dishes in the fridge and freezer for dinners while she would be gone. She left three to the side for personal notes to stick in Theo's and Kelsie's rooms and on Ted's side of the bathroom sink.

Anne adored her family and was very thankful for the blessings of them in her life. She and Ted had met in high school, and they attended

LSU together for college. Her graduation gift was the best she could have hoped for: a marriage proposal and the ring she wore with pride on her left hand. She couldn't imagine her life any other way.

A light honk outside jostled her from her thoughts as she taped Kelsie's note to her door. "I love you! Don't forget your book report is due on Monday," she had written inside a huge heart. After kissing her hand and then patting her daughter's door, she picked up her suitcase and walked out the front door. She noted the seating arrangements with a smile and stowed her suitcase in the trunk, making sure to pull the directions Betty had given her out of her purse to keep handy.

Anne opened the front passenger door and climbed in. "Hi, all! Ready for the retreat?"

"Raring to go!" answered Deli from the back seat.

Once she was settled, Lindsay handed Anne John's napkin. "Perfect," Anne said with a smile as she reached the end of the notes. She showed Lindsay her own paper. "I have directions to the house from 98 once we get to Destin."

Lindsay put the SUV in gear once more. "Next stop, Florida!" she said with an answering chorus of cheers.

With each lady content either with her own thoughts or listening to the radio, Lindsay drove steadily along Scenic Highway 98, past the myriad of pecan orchards. A few steadfast green leaves clung to their color as brown began its yearly dominance. The nuts drooped as if readying themselves for their eventual plunge to the ground for harvesting. Pecans were Alabama's other cash crop.

A few more miles, and they were out of Fairhope proper. "Watch your speed in Summerdale," Anne admonished as Lindsay turned onto Highway 32 a little later. "The office manager at Dr. Rucker's got a ticket by the old flea market last week."

Lindsay glanced at her speedometer and let up on the pedal a bit. The engine slowed by three miles per hour. A moment later, they sailed past a police officer's car without him batting an eyelash.

~~*

About an hour later, Deli pulled out a notepad and pen. "You know we should probably put together some sort of grocery list since meals aren't provided."

"Why don't we start with snacks and then build from there?" Jess asked. "Nothing too involved, though. We don't want to spend time cooking either."

"Surely there's a market somewhere around there where we could pick up some premade meals and then reheat or eat them cold," Lindsay offered with a furrowed brow.

"Oh, that's a good idea!" Jess said. "I was reading somewhere about a family-owned market that's been there forever, right in the middle of Seaside."

"That sounds perfect." Lindsay replied. "We'll get there in plenty of time to do some exploring before we need to be at the chapel for registration.

"I figured we would mostly eat out," Anne said as she turned in the seat a bit to see each of the women.

Deli shook her head. "That's fine for breakfast, but lunch may be iffy. While it's not high season over there, this is the time when the young families and empty nesters go on vacation. It'll still be busy enough that wait times could be an issue. I'd hate to miss any of the sessions."

Jess added, "As for dinner, by the time we finish with the practicums, the last thing we might want to do is eat out. We might be too focused on God to be around a lot of hustle and bustle."

Anne nodded. "I would like to eat out at least once for either lunch or dinner. I've heard the restaurants are all just fabulous, and it would be a shame not to get the whole Seaside experience while we're there."

Deli said, "Very true. From what I understand, they have several in the whole area that are four star, and the others are just as yummy. Why don't we ask some of the locals for a recommendation when we register since we may only get to one."

"That's a great idea, Deli," Anne answered. "They would know the ones that are hype versus the ones they go to. I'll make sure to ask Jane when we pick up our packets." Satisfied, she turned back toward the front. "So, snack list then?"

"I've got a notepad. Y'all call out what you want," Jess said as she pulled out a pen and pad from her satchel.

"Bottled water, definitely," Lindsay said as she glanced in the rear-view mirror.

Jess nodded and looked over at Deli, who added, "FGPs and hummus for me."

Anne turned in her seat, confusion written all over her face. Jess mirrored the look.

Deli glanced at the two of them, a mystified furrow on her own brow, and asked, "What? FGPs, fat girl potato chips—you know, carrots."

Jess cackled as she wrote down Deli's request, saying, "Now, that has to be a first!"

"That's definitely one I haven't heard," Anne chimed in. "Lindsay?"

"I think I remember a floor mate in college saying something along those lines, but it's been a while."

Deli shook her head in surprise. "Oh come on, y'all have never heard that? They're part of the reason I lost all my weight. Carrots are the wonder snack!"

Anne said, "All this talk of food is making me hungry. Can we stop for lunch?"

Deli peered out the window in an effort to find a sign. "Where are we?"

"Looks like Navarre," Lindsay said after a glance at the nav system. "Got any ideas, Deli?"

Deli answered, "Definitely, I know a great restaurant just off the beach. One of my friends did a neat little write-up on it about a year ago. We'll have to go to the beach, so it's a bit of a diversion, but the food and the view are well worth it."

With a good-natured smile, Lindsay said, "Deli, I give you permission to be a back-seat driver!"

Chapter 6

Seaside

The ladies arrived at Betty's beach bungalow with plenty of time to unpack and take a look around Seaside, which pleased Deli's travel-writer side. She always preferred to get the lay of the land before embarking on an activity in a new location. It allowed a familiarity to seep into her words, which captured the essence of her surroundings and made her articles readers' favorites several times over.

Betty had opted to bring the landscape rather than the beach indoors. Eschewing the customary aquas and grays typically found in beach cottages, she instead used a variety of greens, browns, and creams popped by the occasional dash of goldenrod. The furniture was an eclectic mix of antique and transitional, lending the house a charming warmth that hugged rather than shook hands. The result: the perfect Southern welcome.

Deli pulled out her phone and tapped the record icon. Soon after, she began a steady description of their surroundings, her tone one of longstanding use. Lindsay shook her head at the sight, and Jess swatted the phone away from Deli's face.

"Stop!" she ordered with mock severity. "You are not here to work, so put—the—phone—down!"

Deli glanced at Jess then the others. Abashed, she slid the phone back into her pocket. "Sorry," she said sheepishly. "It's just kind of hard to turn off."

Anne grinned. "Well, do! This isn't work. Think of it instead as a minivacation, and treat it accordingly! No work e-mails or work texts while we're here."

Deli agreed with a chuckle.

"Oh, speaking of texts," Lindsay said, pulling out her own phone. "I need to let John know we're here. Knowing him, he might send out the Navy Seals!"

Jess and Anne each followed suit. Deli, not having anyone she needed to advise of her arrival, wandered back out to the porch to sneak a peak at the grounds. Her singlehood had never bothered her before. In fact, it was a boon given her job, but while she did love her job, she wondered if she were missing out on something.

Needing to check in with someone before or after doing something had run against her independent streak, but what if that, like Mary's choice to sit at Jesus's feet, were the better portion? She had never had anyone else to rely on or to take into consideration, so she had never thought she was lacking anything. Yet seeing her friends happily check in with their spouses or boyfriend made her question her own choices.

In reality, she had to admit those choices were limited by her past. The last time a guy had asked her out was during her junior year of college, and she had panicked badly. The memory of her childhood nemesis, Jamie Rogers, and how he had turned on her rushed to the fore and crashed over the sweet request. While she had reluctantly accepted the offer, when the time came for the date, she was petrified that once they were out together, he would switch from a nice guy to a mean-spirited boor who ridiculed her at the first opportunity.

Instead of meeting her date at the restaurant, she had hidden in the library that night and during her free time for the next week, in an effort to avoid him. When the student therapist asked her about the week, she had confessed her reaction, and they had begun to work through the greatest of her fears. However, when she joined the *Tribune*, she made sure to be seen more as one of the guys, so she could safely sidestep any chance of romantic interactions.

Deli shook her head, clearing away the memory, and found that her meandering had led her to the back of the lot. A quartet of brightly colored beach cruisers chained to a bike rack prompted the return of her usual smile. She heard the side door of the house open and called to the others. "Hey, I found our transportation while we're here!"

Jess came around the corner first. "Oh, those are perfect!" she gushed. "I haven't ridden a bike in years."

Lindsay checked out the baskets that were attached to the rear racks. "These will be perfect for bringing back groceries from the market in the square. Why don't we ride over now and get the lay of the area as well as some groceries, then get back in time for registration?"

Anne agreed. "That sounds great. We should have plenty of time for dinner on the beach before the first session."

After more than a bit of wobbling, but at least no tumbles, their bodies were reacquainted with balancing on bicycles, and the quartet set off to the Seaside Central Square.

"Isn't it interesting how none of the picket fences are the same," Jess remarked as they turned down Seaside Avenue.

Anne agreed and added, "Betty said one time when we were talking about the house that it's a rule that was set out by the town's founder. It's fun seeing all of the house names, too. Some of them make you wonder about the story behind them." She pointed at a house across the street and laughed. "The Wright Stuff is owned by David and Sheila Wright. How cute!"

Deli and the others chuckled as they continued to pedal. A few minutes later they reached the middle of Seaside. A bike rack was conveniently placed where the two streets joined. The ladies parked and locked the bikes, then took a quick look around.

Deli noticed that Central Square was a misnomer because it was more of a lower case A than a square, curved on one side with County Highway 30A forming the straight-line closure. In the middle was a huge outdoor amphitheater surrounded by grass and trimmed with a white gravel walkway and towering medjool palm trees. Along the outer rim were the shops and restaurants, many with condos above them.

They walked across the pavers—apparently a distinguishing feature since all the streets in Seaside seemed to have them instead of asphalt—to get a closer look at the amphitheater. Kids and dogs chased each other around the grassy incline while their parents and owners looked on.

"How cool is this?" Lindsay asked rhetorically as she spun around, taking in the whole effect. "Talk about a bit of Nantucket in Florida. Oh! There's the market. It's just down from where we left the bikes."

"So where should we start?" Jess asked, shading her eyes to better see the options. She had left her sunglasses back at the house, and Deli hoped her friend wouldn't make that mistake again. The Florida sun was quite a bit brighter than Fairhope's.

Anne pointed to a mannequin and T-shirt display across the street. "That looks fun! Why don't we start there and work our way back so we won't be carrying a ton of stuff through the stores?"

"Good idea," Deli said. "But knowing Lindsay, she'll end up with bags of stuff anyway!"

Lindsay shot a mock glare toward the other woman. "Hey, I'm not that bad!"

"Yes," Anne said, then added *sotto voce*, "but John did say to keep her at a two-bag minimum!"

"I'm going to pretend I didn't hear that!" Lindsay replied archly. "I'll have you know, the last time I took the girls to Mobile, we came back with only one bag!"

"And how big was the bag?" Jess teased.

Lindsay wrinkled her nose at the question. "We're not going to talk about that!"

Amid peals of laughter, the ladies walked though the door into the Trading Post and stepped into cowgirl heaven. Lindsay spied something in the cubby display of T-shirts and rushed over. "Just for that comment, John is getting this T-shirt!" she said as she held up a faded-blue vintage shirt with "Trophy Husband" printed on the front. Anne nearly doubled over in laughter, envisioning John wearing the shirt and knowing, with his sense of humor, he would do so proudly.

Deli and Jess had slipped past them, drawn to the display of assorted hats. They began trying out different styles and posing in the full-length mirror. The saleswoman smiled and offered opinions, but each happily denied any real interest and began roaming the racks while Lindsay paid for the shirt.

As they left the store, Anne spotted two kids' stores and urged Lindsay to come with her. "I won't hear the end of it if I don't bring Theo something back, and I'd love to get Kelsie something educational."

Deli elbowed Jess as she saw a bookstore further down the way. "I'm heading there. The writer in me can never pass up a good bookstore." Seeing Anne's warning glare reminding her of the directive to avoid work, she added, "It's a love; it's not work. I promise!"

Anne giggled at the plea and encouraged Deli on. "I think I'll keep Deli company," Jess said. "I can probably find Mitch a book about the town. I'm sure he'd love to read about how they chose this architecture." She glanced further down and added, "Why don't we meet y'all at the market?"

"Great! Take your time browsing. I'm sure we'll be a while!" Anne answered, sending them off with a wave as she trailed Lindsay into the toy store.

"Oh, this looks fun," Deli said as they passed a Florida cracker-style restaurant with a wraparound porch and a chalkboard claiming the best mojitos on 30A.

"Certainly smells good," Jess commented. "Maybe we should ask about it at registration."

Deli nodded but continued on to their original destination. Words rather than food occupied her mind for the moment.

They climbed the gray wooden steps and walked through the open door. Flyers plastered to the window announced everything from upcoming book signings to area concerts. The heady scent of paper and ink slammed into Deli's senses, and a feeling of homecoming unfurled within her. As a kid and even into her college years, the library had been her favorite haunt. All the possibilities. All the dreams. With a contented sigh, she told Jess, "That's it. You can leave me here. I'll be happy for the rest of the weekend." Jess shook her head with a laugh and squeezed past her to check out the greeting cards in the racks along the window.

Deli walked the length of the new release table, her fingers caressing the hardbacks as she passed by, intent on the "staff favorites" section. She felt the plywood sheet floor give a bit under her sandaled feet. The well-worn paint from the heavy foot traffic of the vacationers and locals spoke volumes as to the store's popularity. In the background, Nina Simone's throaty wail serenaded customers with tales of love and loss. In the foreground were tall bookshelves packed with options and categorized by hand-drawn signs. The wide aisles that would be claustrophobic in high season now held only a handful of people stocking up on reading material for their beach days.

Deli's winding tour led her to the back of the store, where T-shirts, mugs, and lidded cups lined the walls. A tie-dyed short-sleeve shirt with the store's logo on the back caught her eye. Selecting her size, she pulled off the rubber band that held it rolled tightly and raised it to her front. She glanced back into the main part of the store, found Jess lingering at a table of books about the area, and called, "What do you think? Is it me?" Deli's stark black hair could change to match any one of the colors in the shirt at the drop of hat.

Jess nodded with an enthusiastic grin and gave her a thumbs-up. "I don't think anything could be more you!"

Deli gestured widely. "Right?" she answered with a chuckle. "Okay, found my souvenir. What about you and Mitch?" she asked as she walked back toward Jess.

Jess tapped one of the books on the architecture of Seaside and said, "I'm thinking this would be right up his alley. Mitch would love to see all the architectural features in the area. He would probably get a boatload of ideas for his next build in just five minutes."

"Go for it," Deli said. She paused and then broached a subject she had been wondering about for a while. "So, any chance the next house he'll build will be for the two of you?"

Jess looked up quickly, apparently startled by the question.

"Ohhhkay," Deli breathed, "so I'm guessing that's a no."

Jess sighed and shook her head. "Oh, I don't know. He's wonderful, and I can see us being married, but I just can't get past his less-than-enthusiastic faith."

Deli winced. She knew Jess's faith was the most important thing in her life and for her boyfriend not to share that had to be tough for her. "I'm sorry, Jess. I didn't mean to hit a sore spot."

Jess gave her a wan smile. "Not your fault. In fact, it was a question I was hoping to find an answer to this weekend. Mitch has been broadly hinting that he wants us to get married sometime soon, but I change the subject as quickly as I can." She picked up a book on the local bird populations and leafed through it without appearing to read one word on any of the pages. "The kicker is I do love him."

"But can you marry a man who doesn't love God first?" Deli asked.

Jess nodded sadly.

"Yeah, that's a toughie. Well, let's just pray that God has some insight for you this weekend."

A flash of color caught Deli's eye through the open front door, and she saw Lindsay and Anne, multiple bags between them, hurrying toward the market. Deli gave Jess's forearm a squeeze and said, "Looks like Anne and Lindsay will beat us. Better check out and get to the store."

Jess nodded with a quick smile, picked up her original choice for Mitch, and headed to the checkout counter.

~~*

The Seaside Market, family owned since almost the beginning of Seaside itself, was a mainstay and a must-do pit stop for all comers. Part sundries, part deli, part wine and beer hall, it catered to all needs a body could have and was the place for vacationers to feel most like locals. The modern-day general store's corrugated metal exterior and artfully drawn poster announcement of the daily specials radiated a chic casual appeal. The four-top tables outside—strategically positioned for dining, shooting the breeze, people-watching, or all of the above—were accented by a handful of sparrows hopping about, eager to nab the slightest fallen crumb. Delighted at the heavier tidbits tossed by the patrons, they swarmed the offering, the luckiest few actually able to peck away at it.

Shopping list torn into fourths, the ladies separated, each intent on her assigned selections. Sunlight streamed through the skylight on one side of the room, highlighting the wall of wines. Lindsay skipped that section and instead peered through the glass of the deli cases at the ready-made take-away offerings. Selecting pints of salads and a few sandwiches, she asked for a couple to be made up into lettuce wraps, which was readily accommodated with a bit of a wait.

Jess stood at the other side of the counter, which held the baked goods section, and selected an assortment of muffins. Anne remained around the corner with the fresh veggies and canned goods, while Deli grabbed the drinks and dry goods. A few minutes later, they regrouped at the register.

"How do you want these rung up?" the cashier asked.

Deli, who was first in line, suggested, "Why don't we split it as is? I'm sure it'll all come out in the wash."

The others agreed, and the cashier began to run the items through. "So where are y'all in from?" she asked in a friendly, expectant tone.

Jess, now next in line as Deli ran her credit card through, answered, "We're from Fairhope and came over for the Courtyard Chapel's retreat."

"Oh, that's great!" the cashier beamed. "The pastor regularly comes and sits at the tables outside with his Bible. You should hear some of the conversations that get started out there."

"I'm sure they're quite interesting!" Anne said.

The cashier nodded. "Even though this is the Bible belt's Riviera, we get all types in here. Some have a deep faith, some are Christian in name only, and some are full-on something else. Doesn't matter a bit to Greg. He loves them all and talks as much or as little as they can handle."

Jess's smile warmed at the comment. "Sounds like he's the perfect pastor for this area then."

"He's definitely found his niche, that's for sure," the cashier commented as she scanned Anne's selections.

With all the goods paid for, the ladies thanked the cashier and headed back to the bikes. Unfortunately, none of them had anticipated the impact of the added weight in the baskets when they first rode over and more laughter and wobbles accompanied the ride home than the ride there.

~~*

"Wow, some turnout, huh?" Kaci Steele asked Jane as she dropped into the empty folding chair next to the pastor's wife, who sat behind a card table laden with packets and binders.

Jane agreed. "I never dreamed we would have more than a dozen people since I'm lucky to have that many for the Bible studies. But to have thirty! That is, if everyone comes." She looked at the diminishing stacks of materials and estimated that about two thirds were already taken. It was only four thirty, and registration lasted until six o'clock. Given those numbers, she crossed her fingers that there wouldn't be a large attrition rate. Just as she was about to share her thoughts with Kaci, a group of four ladies walked up. She smiled up at them and asked, "Are you here for the retreat?"

"Yes, we're the group from Fairhope," the redhead answered. She quickly introduced the group, "Anne Greeley, Lindsay Davenport, Jess McAdams, and Deli Preston."

"Oh yes, Anne!" Jane beamed. "So glad y'all could make it. Welcome! You'll each need a name tag, a binder, and a pen." As each lady collected her supplies, Jane happily gushed, "Is this your first visit to Seaside? Do you have any questions about the area?"

Jess raised her hand slightly. "We were wondering about some of the local restaurants. We just bought some basics at the Seaside Market, but do you have any recommendations for dinner?"

"Heavens, yes!" Jane said. "The restaurants around here are all just top-notch. Now, if you're wanting something quick and easy, I'd recommend the Airstreams. They sell food-truck food, and it's absolutely yummy—perfect to grab and go sit on the beach if that's where your interest lies." Seeing the nods of the other two ladies, she added, "Now, if it's sit-down you're wanting, you can't beat Southern Kitchen."

Deli tapped Jess on the arm and said, "That's the one we passed by on the way to the bookstore."

Jane nodded. "That's right. They have the best Southern food going, and their key lime pie is the best on 30A!" She grinned then added a word of caution. "Now, keep in mind, the wait times around here get a little long, and while it's not high season anymore, there's still enough people in town to make it interesting. They do serve a marvelous breakfast as well."

"What is lunch around here like?" Jess asked.

"Oh, we decided to add in a boxed lunch both days," Jane answered. "It will give everyone the opportunity to ask Mary questions about the activities before getting into them in the next session. Plus, the weather is supposed to be lovely all weekend, and our green and courtyard are the perfect places for a picnic."

"That's a great idea," Lindsay agreed. "So, why don't we go to Southern Kitchen for breakfast one morning and scope out the dinner menu for later?"

Anne agreed. "That sounds like the best plan, Lindsay. Let's grab some dinner tonight at the Airstreams and then head over to the beach to watch the sunset."

"That sounds perfect to me," Jess replied.

"What time is sunset now?" Deli asked. "I don't want to be late to the first session."

Jane nodded at her wisdom. "It's been setting about five or ten till seven here lately, so I'd say you'll probably need to leave a bit early, given it's a good ten-minute walk from the beach to here."

"Excellent!" Lindsay answered. "Beach time and a sunset sound like the perfect way to get ready for a retreat."

Anne and the others nodded. "Thanks so much for all your help, Jane. We'll see you back here a little before seven then!"

Jane cheerfully waved them on and, with no sign of any other impending arrival, turned to Kaci quietly taking in the conversation from the seat beside her. "So, how are the kids settling back in? I know it has to be hard on you sending them back to Texas after having them for the summer."

Kaci nodded. She was a divorcée with two kids, a fifteen-year-old daughter and a ten-year-old son, who lived with their father in Dallas during the school year. The children came to stay with her during the summer. Jane knew Kaci's life as a successful singer and songwriter took her on the road too often to give them the stability they needed. "It is hard," she agreed, "but I know the choices I've made for my career. I've accepted that our relationship is going to be different from those of other mothers and children."

"At least you and Bobby have been able to work out a schedule that you both can live with, given the distance."

"That is a tremendous blessing," Kaci agreed. "I don't know of many people who have as good a relationship with their exes as I have with Bobby, and I call and text the kids all the time when they aren't here. They know I love them, and they support my career, but they're also very glad not to be moved from here to there and have private tutors and no friends their age. Life on the road would be tough for them, especially Monica. She's such a social butterfly."

"Thank you again so much for taking time out of your schedule to lead the worship," Jane said. "Matt would be happy to do it, but I thought since it's a women's retreat, he would stick out like a sore thumb, even though he's our weekly worship pastor."

Kaci shook her head with a smile. "It's not a problem at all. I'm so glad you asked me."

"So how long are you here this time?"

"Oh, next week I'll have to take a short trip up to New York for a concert and then hit Nashville on the way back to check in with the record label, but then I'll be here for at least a month. My manager can't understand why I don't want to be in the center of everything and stay closer to where I work, but I just love the artsy feel of this area. I can't tell you how many songs I have written in that carriage house."

Jane laughed. "I think it's the sea air!"

Kaci joined her laughter and answered, "You're probably right." She leaned forward to check out two more ladies approaching the chapel. "Looks like we have more incoming!"

Chapter 7

Mary Black stood at the front of the Courtyard Chapel and silently counted heads. With little more than five minutes before seven, all but a couple of the ladies were present. *Lord, help me to teach them Your word so they are better able to study and absorb it for themselves,* she silently prayed as the last two women found their seats.

With a nod to Jane, who sat in the front row, ready to give the introductions, Mary released any lingering flutterings of nerves and firmly grabbed hold of Jesus's hand. Jane rose and took the hand mic from the stand and said, "I want to officially welcome each of you to the Courtyard Chapel's first-ever women's retreat. We are honored to have two very special ladies here to help us this weekend." She gestured to Kaci, who stood at the music stand, guitar at the ready. "Let me introduce Kaci Steele. She's a singer and songwriter out of Nashville, but makes her home here in Seacrest Beach. Kaci will be leading us in worship tonight and prior to each teaching session. Kaci?"

The singer smiled at Jane in thanks and then turned her gaze to the group. "Ladies, if you'll stand and turn to the first sheet in your binders, we'll begin with Chris Tomlin's 'Amazing Grace.'"

The strum of the guitar strings soon filled the chapel, and Kaci's throaty alto was joined by voices of all ranges and abilities. When the final words died, she smoothly changed chords and moved into Bethel Music's version of "It is Well." When she, Jane, and Kaci had first sat down to plan the retreat, they had decided on only two songs each session, but Mary had given Kaci free rein in the song selection. She found Kaci's choices of songs for that night as well as the rest of the weekend perfect to set the mood and invite the Holy Spirit to join their gathering. Kaci would be a wonderful worship leader if she ever decided to leave the secular stage.

Jane stepped forward again as Kaci allowed the D chord of the chorus to fade and encouraged the ladies to take their seats. "Thank you so much, Kaci!" she said as the singer took her seat. "Now, may I introduce our speaker for the weekend. Mary Black comes to us from just outside of Nashville and is a gifted speaker and Bible study leader. She brings clear insight and an open heart to all of her seminars and retreats, and I'm very excited to see what she has for us this weekend!"

Polite applause filled the room as Mary stepped forward and turned up the headset of her body mic. She had set up her notes on a music stand prior to the session and was all set to begin. "Thank you so much," she said as she glanced around the room. "I am so excited to have this opportunity to teach on two of my favorite ways to study Scripture. First off, though, let me tell you I think of my teaching time as less lecture and more forum. I believe interaction is the key to retaining new information. So if you have any questions or if something is unclear, raise your hand and ask. There are no silly questions in my book."

A chuckle flitted through the group. Mary raised a staying hand and added, "But I will say, I reserve the right to move on and discuss the question in further detail at lunch if it looks to be one that is too in-depth for the time we have allotted." Understanding nods signaled the ladies' acceptance of the rule.

"This weekend is going to be a workout. Day one we'll focus on building your faith. Day two will stretch and deepen your understanding of Scripture. So for those of you who thought you were going to relax this weekend, I'm sorry to disappoint you. However, I am praying that by the end of the weekend you'll feel a closer intimacy and connection to God, which is really what we all want, right?

"To accomplish this, we will be using two different methods for studying Scripture. We'll begin with reflection tomorrow morning and move into meditation on Saturday. I know that those two words can bring to mind tattooed people sitting cross-legged on the floor while intoning odd chants, but reflection and meditation are actually biblically based methods for studying the Word of God.

"With reflection, we take a verse and basically mull over it to determine how it is evident in our lives. The meditation teaching will be a more in-depth method of studying Scripture. We will be taking the actual meanings of certain key words and meditating on the context in order to get the full impact of the Scripture. Through reflection and meditation, we can encounter God in a deeper way so, in our lives and on the paths we walk, He will be our source and our guide.

"I see you each received a binder with blank paper as well as the lyrics for the worship songs we'll be singing this weekend. You'll need to bring these with you to every session. In the teaching sessions, you'll likely want to take notes to help you remember what we talked about when you get to the practicum sessions. During the practicum sessions, you'll need them for jotting down insights as well as completing the word studies for your personal verses.

"For the reflection portion, we will each study the same verse. For the meditation, I have selected thirty verses that you'll each choose from and then complete the activity from there. The word study list will be handed out after lunch on Saturday and right before you're dismissed to the practicum portion. So, no working ahead, you overachievers! The final outcome is a greater insight into God's Word and how your life exemplifies it. Sound good?" she asked with an inviting grin.

An agreeable murmur rippled back to her.

"That's it for tonight. You are dismissed, and we'll see you back in here in the morning. Nine sharp!"

Mary smiled as the ladies rose and collected their belongings. Through the competing conversations she caught a few of the plans for the evening. Some were headed to Seaside for dinner, and a few others were going back to their homes. All in all, it would be a quiet night. She was pleased that the group seemed to be serious about the weekend and ready to learn. A quick prayer of blessing for restful evenings, and she headed home for her own quiet reflection.

Chapter 8

Contrary to what Deli had said about not being an early riser, Friday morning she found herself out of bed and dressed in her running gear by six thirty. She had slept so well the night before that there was no reason to linger in bed, especially as their first session began at nine. Perhaps it was because this was truly a minivacation rather than yet another exotic place to analyze in detail for later description. This time, as her friends had said, she got to turn off work mode and just relax.

Grabbing a bottle of water, she studied the map that Jane had given them in each of their registration packets and mapped out a circuitous route that would keep her in the general area of the house and chapel. She jotted a note to the others and left it on the kitchen counter, then stepped onto the porch and quietly shut the front door behind her.

A cool hint of autumn lurked in the warmth of the sea breeze. Like the lightest top note of a perfume, it wafted away to reveal the deeper, heavier notes of summer's heat and humidity. Deli paused to breathe in the salted air, familiar and yet much different from her most recent exposure in the Caribbean, given the added aromas of the long leaf and sand pines. She would be hard-pressed to deny that those additions heightened the natural beauty around her. It would seem the orange and black butterflies that flitted around the native lantana bushes agreed with her. She watched two members of the group twirl around each other in a butterfly tornado and smiled at their antics.

With a final glance at her map, she zipped it up in a pocket on her running shorts, tapped shuffle on her "Run" playlist, and slipped in her earbuds. After a couple of light quad and hamstring stretches, she was off.

Deli headed west toward the chapel and skirted around the tennis courts, heading for WaterColor, the community that bordered Seaside, and the gravel trails that wove around Western Lake. Steady, even breathing and equally steady footfalls were accented by the beat of Toby Mac. However, her first turn on the trail stuttered her steps, almost stopping her in her tracks. Western Lake peeked through the pines, and scrub oaks basked in the buttercream yellow of the rising sun. Each leaf seemed to dance and shimmer as the glow of the morning met them, accenting their perfection. Even the water, now glass dotted with lily pads and native grasses, seemed to radiate a welcome of the morning. The view was breathtaking.

Her attention was soon recaptured as she reached the narrowest footbridge, barely one-person width across. She slowed her pace as the bridge twisted over lowland and through a heavy conglomeration of saw palmettos, scrub oaks, and long leaf pines. About a yard further along, she was again greeted by a bridge, albeit wider, but paused anyway. Two bicyclists were also out enjoying the morning. She gave way to them and glanced back out at the lake.

Her gaze caught at the sight of someone paddleboarding out on the water. Deli watched him for a moment, then nodded to the cyclists as they passed and returned to her run. As she reached the rise, the paddleboarder returned to her line of sight, and the smooth, easy strokes as he glided across the glass top of the lake mesmerized her.

For a little while, it seemed as if they were each keeping time: one stroke per two footfalls. Deli could hear her breathing ramp up as she reached a graduated incline. Though it was not nearly as steep as the hill in Fairhope, the gravel and loose sand made the path slicker and forced her to turn her attention from the paddleboarder to her own progress.

In her earbuds, the Toby montage merged into the smooth drive of Lacrae as she once more glanced out toward the lake. The paddleboarder was replaced by the view of a wide bridge that spanned the width of Western Lake. A few strides later, the path opened to a green edged by buildings in the same coastal architecture as the houses that dotted the length of the trail.

Curious as to where the bridge over the lake began, she slowed to a walk and glanced around to her right. She spied another runner coming from the north, just a little way over, and decided that was the most likely location for the bridge. Her supposition was soon confirmed as she reached the timber sidewalk that led onto the expanse.

Multicolored glass cattails lined the bridge entrance and enhanced the lake's natural beauty. To her left, she found a boathouse lined with paddleboards, likely the place the paddler had put in for his paddle.

As Deli reached the middle of the bridge, she once again found the paddleboarder. She leaned against the bridge railing, hands clasped around her water bottle, and watched him as he made the turn around the yellow buoy just past the pier and headed back toward the boathouse. He apparently sensed her interest and ended his run standing near the side of the pier closest to her.

"Good morning!" he greeted. His low-country drawl innate to native South Carolinians was like melted chocolate—sweet, smooth, and thick. "You eveh been on a board?"

Deli shook her head. "No, but it looks really peaceful."

He chuckled good-naturedly. "It can be, but you should see the races. They get to be quite lively."

She smiled in response and added a soft, "I'll bet." She shivered as his accent slipped over her, warming her more than the sun rapidly rising behind her. Yet while one lulled, the other startled and woke her just as effectively as a reveille bugle. The increasing light reminded her that she was running out of time. She glanced at her phone in the armband on her bicep and confirmed the sun's timing. With a rueful shake of her head, she said, "I have to go. I, um, I have a thing to get to."

"Yeah, I've a meeting myself. It'll last most of the day, but I could meet you back here, say around four? Be more than happy to teach you." She watched his lips turn up into a smile. If she thought his voice was warming, that charmingly boyish grin could easily ignite a forest fire.

Deli blinked and opened her mouth. When no words came out, she closed it, only to find it opening once more with words of acceptance falling out of it. "Um, yeah, okay." His grin gained wattage. "I, um, yeah, I—" she stammered and randomly pointed behind her.

"You've got to go," he interpreted. "Yeah, I got that." He leaned slightly against his paddle as he braced himself on the board. She turned, suddenly panicked by the change in the conversation. "But I'll see you later!" he called to her back. Deli couldn't answer.

~~*

Anne was handing Lindsay a mug for her tea when the front door opened, revealing Deli. The woman looked worse for the wear between her sweat-soaked running shirt and pale, panicked brow. Stunned, neither she nor Lindsay nor Jess could form any words. None of them had ever seen Deli in such a state.

Deli bit her lip, then, as if she suddenly realized she wasn't alone, glanced over to her friends. Before anyone could speak, she dashed up the stairs and slammed her bedroom door behind her.

The slamming door jolted the women back to their senses. "What in the world happened to her?" Jess asked, mystified. "Her note said she was just going for a run."

Lindsay nodded. "Yeah, something else must have happened on that run. But she didn't look hurt or even scraped, so she couldn't have taken a fall."

Anne said, "I'll go check on her." She flashed a rueful smile and added, "Trust me. I have plenty of experience talking to a girl through a bedroom door." She quietly moved up the stairs so as not to startle Deli and called before she reached the door, "Deli, honey, what happened?"

No answer. Anne moved closer to the door and could hear Deli gasping for breath. "Slow down, Deli. You'll hyperventilate and pass out. Breathe in slowly and then out just as slowly." When Deli's breathing continued at its rapid pace, Anne prompted, "Come on, Del. Slow down. Breathe with me." Anne inhaled slowly then slipped the air out through her pursed lips at the same rate. A few breaths later, Deli's rate had slowed.

"Good girl," Anne said soothingly. "Now, tell me what happened." When the silence continued, she asked, "Can you at least open the door? We're really worried about you. I need to make sure you're not hurt."

Anne heard a shuffling movement and watched as the door handle turned. She waved Lindsay and Jess up and eased open the door. Deli sat on the floor, still mostly pale, but with the beginnings of color returning to her cheeks. Anne slid a hand over her forehead to check for a temperature and then gave her debris-free clothes a once-over. Noting her unmarked skin, she decided Deli hadn't fallen or hurt herself physically, so it was all emotional. Anne pursed her lips. Unfortunately, that was often harder to deal with than cuts and bruises.

She heard Jess and Lindsay come in. “Why don’t we get her off the floor and on her bed?” Anne asked the others in her most soothing mothering voice. They quickly complied, and between the three of them, they were able to ease Deli to a standing position and sit her on the bed. Jess and Lindsay stationed themselves on either side of her, an arm wrapped around each side, while Anne grabbed the Windsor chair in the corner to sit in front of her and chafed Deli’s cold hands.

“Okay, sweetie, ’fess up,” Jess said. “What happened that’s got you so freaked out?”

Deli’s eyes focused at Jess’s question, and she swallowed audibly. “He, um, he—” her voice cracked. Clearing her throat, she continued haltingly, “He’s perfect. And he asked me if I wanted to learn how to paddleboard.”

Lindsay’s eyebrows shot up almost even with her hairline. Anne, too, was surprised that this was about a guy. Then she remembered Deli’s history. It was easy to forget in light of the lovely and confident young woman she knew her to be that Deli had been horribly bullied as a child over her weight. It shouldn’t have surprised her that the woman would have social anxiety with the opposite sex. Given her reaction though, this must have been quite a guy.

Anne gave Lindsay an encouraging nod. Lindsay squeezed Deli’s shoulder in support, then prompted, “Tell us the whole story, Deli. Then we can talk it out and come up with a solution.”

Deli nodded absently and cleared her throat again. She looked at Anne with a plea in her eyes. Correctly reading that she needed water, Anne picked up the water bottle that had rolled over by the closet when Deli had collapsed on the floor. A quick twist, and Deli was gulping greedily. A few swallows later, she lowered the bottle and wiped her mouth on her sleeve. She shot Anne a thankful smile and then nodded as if collecting her scattered thoughts and emotions.

“Okay. I went running this morning, as y’all know. And I took the trails in the community behind the chapel. They run along Western Lake. As I was running, I saw this person paddleboarding, and it was just beautiful—the water like glass, and the sun rising over the trees.” She paused, and Anne offered a supportive smile and squeezed Deli’s now warmed hands. “Well, I got to a bridge, and it was too pretty not to stop and say a thank-you to God, you know? And then he was still there, still paddling. So I stood and watched him. It was mesmerizing. There was something about that moment that I knew in my bones was special." She paused again.

Anne felt a warmth creep over her skin. Deli had experienced a pure and perfect God moment, and she had a sneaking suspicion that it was merely the first. "Keep going," she urged.

Deli nodded. Then, as if she could hardly believe it herself, she whispered, "When he got to the bridge, he looked up and smiled at me, and when he spoke, oh God, he had the most beautiful accent. Has to be from somewhere in South Carolina. It just kind of rumbled through me." She trailed off, lost in the memory. A shiver crossed her skin, and Jess and Lindsay hugged her tighter, a smile beginning to tip the corners of Lindsay's lips.

"So, what did he say?" Jess asked, eyes alight at the possibilities

Deli half chuckled, half sighed. "He asked me if I knew how to paddleboard. I told him no, and he offered to teach me this afternoon." Panic once again glazed her eyes, and she slumped over, her head landing in Anne's lap. A tremble rippled through her shoulders. "Oh, but there's no way I can go!" she cried.

Anne ran a soothing hand over Deli's back and swapped proud, understanding smiles with the others. "What do you mean you can't go?" Anne pulled Deli back up to a seated position. "Of course you can go! The third session of the retreat will be over by then, and we're on our own for dinner. There's absolutely nothing keeping you from going."

A pained expression stole over Deli's face as she wailed, "I don't know what I'll say!"

Anne swallowed an involuntary giggle at her usually steady friend's dramatic response. Now was not the time for teasing. Deli had a history of real pain to back up her fear. Anne squeezed the hands she still clasped. "You're a travel writer," she reminded her. "I'm sure you have to talk to men on an almost daily basis."

Deli shook her head, panic creeping back into her brown eyes. "That's completely different. I'm in work mode and have specific topics or details that I need to get. This is social, and I absolutely implode here."

"Well, you can't just not show up. That would be horribly rude," Lindsay countered with practical Southern logic. "Besides, who's to say this isn't divinely arranged?"

Jess nodded. "You have to admit, it does sound a lot like something God would do."

"I'm not ready for this. I'm not even looking!" Deli cried. She shook her head then turned her face into Lindsay's shoulder and mumbled, "And I'm scared. What if he turns on me like Jamie did? I liked him so much, and he became my worst nightmare."

"Oh, honey," Lindsay said as she wrapped both arms around her friend. "First off, Jamie was a child. As were you. This is a man, and you are a successful, confident woman with many talents."

"And to top that, you have your faith to support you," Jess added.

Lindsay gave her a comforting squeeze. "If it helps take off some pressure, think of this meeting as just a time to practice. It's like when my girls learn a new dance sequence. The teacher shows them what to do and they learn how to do it, but their moves aren't smooth and natural until after they've practiced over and over again. You already know what to do because you've seen people date on TV and in life. Now it's time for you to use those skills and polish your own movements. You just have trust the Holy Spirit to give you the words."

Delia raised uncertain eyes to meet Lindsay's steady, empathetic gaze. "And if it is God, you'll know. I promise. It'll be easy. You'll know exactly what to say without even thinking about it. That was how I met John."

Seeing Deli had calmed a bit, Anne squeezed her hands once more and said, "You need to grab a shower and some breakfast. I'm sure that will help with some perspective." She gave her a compassionate smile and, with quick check of the clock on the end table, cautioned, "But don't take too long. We have to be at the chapel in forty-five minutes."

Jess patted Deli's leg as she rose off the bed. "Do you need help with anything? Want me to lay out some clothes?"

Deli wiped the tears from her cheeks and shook her head. "No, it'll give me something else to focus on, but thank you, and thank all of you for being here. I'm so sorry I wigged out like this."

Lindsay placed a comforting hand on Deli's arm. "Nothing

to apologize for. We all have our wounds, and sometimes they get triggered." Anne's gaze zeroed in on Lindsay, who shrugged slightly and, flashing an abashed smile, turned back to Deli. "That's why we need people to lean on from time to time."

Deli gave Lindsay a watery smile and hugged each woman in turn. Then, with a resolute nod, she shooed them out the door. "I'll be down in a few minutes."

Chapter 9

The first five rows of pews were again filled with ladies, and Mary was pleased that all thirty had returned, binders in hand and pens at the ready. She took a fortifying breath as Kaci found her seat after the worship segment and offered a welcoming smile. "It's good to see everyone back, bright eyed and bushy tailed! So let's get started. Jane will be passing out the handouts for this morning's session so you can follow along."

Giving Jane a few minutes to distribute the papers, Mary settled on the high bar stool next to the music stand that held her notes and water bottle. She gave the ladies a moment to glance at the notes, then began.

"Reflection is a way to look back and see God's fingerprints on your life. It allows you to see that He was there in the pain and in the joy. It's a faith builder because as you see how He was with you in those times, it will deepen your trust that He is already there in the coming times, ready to guide and comfort. In turn, this gives you the confidence to step more boldly into what He has for you.

"When you take a Scripture, listen for the Holy Spirit to prompt you with memories. He'll drop little seeds in the form of words or pictures during your time of reflection that will expand your understanding and awareness of His presence in your life. So how do we do this? We go back to the simple formula of the Five Ws and one H: who, what, when, where, why and how." She paused to allow the group to absorb the technique and jot down notes to help them process it.

"First we start with simply reading the passage slowly. Then you'll read it again, but this time aloud. Once you have it sufficiently in your working memory, it's time to begin asking questions. It doesn't matter which one you start with, but here are some examples: When was this true for me? Where was I? What are some examples from that time? Who was with me or involved, if anyone? Why is God showing me this verse? What does He want me to either see or learn? How was He always there? How will I move forward with this knowledge?" Mary paused again as several of the ladies were writing furiously, and she repeated two of the sample questions when asked.

"This is not something to be rushed, and you may find yourself reflecting on one verse over the course of several days until you get a full picture. Then there may be times when not all the questions will apply or even be answerable until later, but you've built a foundation to return to, and you can fill in those hidden pieces as they make themselves known to you." Mary waited a moment to allow the information to sink in and to provide time for any further questions before continuing on.

Seeing everyone was attentive and appeared to be clear on the information, she stated, "Let's try a practice verse I've selected. I'll use an example from my own life to show you what came to me when I reflected on this verse. Then we're going to take a few minutes during which I'd like each of you to think of your current situation and how it relates to the verse. Jot down your insights, and then I'll ask for volunteers to share what they learned. Please remember, there are no right or wrong answers. This is a very personalized activity."

Mary opened her Bible where it had been bookmarked and then read the verse, "'Cast your cares on the Lord and he will sustain you; he will never let the righteous be shaken.' Psalm 55:22 in the NIV." Mary waited a moment so the verse could sink into each person. "When I was preparing for our time together, the Lord led me to this verse as a reminder of a time when I leaned heavily on Him. I was married for fourteen years to Len. We weren't saved when we met and married. A coworker of mine led me to Christ when we had been married about five years. Len wasn't interested and would become irritable when I brought up my salvation. He didn't mind that I was, as he would say, 'into all that Jesus stuff,' but he didn't want any part of it for himself."

She smiled slightly at the memory. "Now, what does any good Christian wife do in a situation like that?" she asked rhetorically. "She prays for her husband's heart to soften." Mary paused, hearing the understanding chuckles. "So when we go back and look at the verse, we have found my *care*. And how did I cast it on the Lord? Through prayer.

"Now comes the next part of the verse: 'he will sustain you.' As you might remember, I was saved five years into our fourteen-year marriage. Never once during that time did I have any doubt that Len would come into his own faith. I just knew it in my bones that my prayers were being heard, but was there an obvious sign?" She shook her head. "Nope. He didn't ask about church, never went with me to church, and he changed the channel as soon as he possibly could when a preacher came on TV. In every aspect of the natural world, nothing was being accomplished, but God sustained me. About ten years into our marriage and at the bleakest point in my prayers, I had a dream of God writing Len's name in the Book of Life."

She smiled at the tearful faces of a few of the ladies. "Four years after that, we had a terrible snowstorm in Nashville, and Len was driving home from work when the worst of it hit. His car was T-boned by an SUV that had lost control on the ice." She hesitated, the memory still as fresh as it was that day, and took a deep breath. A hush fell over the chapel as if the ladies knew what would be coming next.

"By the time the EMTs were able to get to him, Len was in really bad shape, and he died en route to the hospital. I got the call that he had been in an accident and rushed to the ER.

"Now, remember, the verse says, 'he won't let the righteous be shaken.' When I arrived, I was taken back immediately, and the nurse told me that Len had died in the ambulance on the way there. As you would expect, I was devastated. Not only had my husband died, but I was sure he wouldn't be with me in heaven. It looked as if every prayer I had prayed over the last fourteen years—let alone the vision God had given me—was wrong.

"Somehow I was able to tell the nurse that I wanted to see him, and so she told me his room number and I headed that way. Before I reached Len's room, I saw the EMT who had been in the back of the ambulance with him standing next to the nurse's station, obviously shaken. He saw me about to go in to the room, and he grabbed my arm.

"I will never forget what he told me for as long as I live. He said that in the ambulance, Len was conscious and had asked how bad he was.

The EMT had told him that he'd lost a significant amount of blood and that he was dying, but they were driving as fast as they could to get him help. The EMT said Len just shook his head and asked him if he was a Christian. The EMT told him yes. Len said that his wife was as well and that if he was dying, he wanted to do so with a clean conscience. The EMT said Len could tell him anything he needed to, but Len said, 'No, I need you to do something for me. I want you to pray with me for me to be saved.' The EMT did, and he said he felt God right there in the back of the ambulance. After Len prayed, he asked the EMT, 'Is that all?' and the EMT said, 'That's it.' Then he said Len whispered, 'That's good,' then closed his eyes with a smile and died."

Mary looked through her own tear-filled eyes to find no other dry eye in the chapel. She hadn't shared that story in any of her other seminars—not for a lack of desire, but mainly because she had never felt released by God to do so. *There must be someone here who needed to hear it,* she mused as she grabbed a tissue to dab her eyes.

"And so in that moment, as sad as it was, the righteous were not shaken." She cleared her throat and took a sip of water before continuing. "Now, I'm not expecting any of your situations to be that dramatic," she said and was comforted by the chuckles. "That being said, you should each be able to find situations that you have faced that you could apply as you reflect on this verse. Jane has notecards for each of you to take with you, and I would encourage you to use the blank paper in the binders to write any insights. We'll take about twenty minutes for you to do the activity, and then we'll come back and share. If you want to go and sit out in the courtyard or on the green, feel free. Also, this would be a good time for a bathroom break."

As the ladies gathered their things, some moving to pews further back and others electing to go outside, Mary took another drink of her water and smiled at Jane, who sat in the front pew, slightly stunned. Jane found her voice a moment later as Mary came to sit beside her. "Mary, I had no idea when you told me you were a widow that—" Jane lost what words she had previously found.

Mary nodded and whispered, "I don't share it with many people, because it is so personal. Even though it's the biggest answered prayer in my life thus far, it has been too precious to release."

"Why now?" Jane asked.

"When I was selecting verses and working on my notes, I just heard God tell me it was time. So there must be someone here who needed to hear it, for whatever reason."

~~*

Anne smiled at the other ladies as they separated to begin their practice reflections; each chose a different location for their ponderings. While Deli and Jess decided to stay in the chapel, she and Lindsay headed outside, Lindsay for the park across the street and Anne for the benches in the courtyard.

Anne tapped the index card against her thigh as she walked and mentally repeated the verse over and over. *Cast your cares on the Lord and He will sustain you; He will never let the righteous be shaken. Cast your cares on the Lord and He will sustain you; He will never let the righteous be shaken.*

That's the sticking point, she thought. She had prayed over and over and it seemed like her prayers weren't making it out of the room, let alone up to the throne room—at least where Kelsie, her greatest worry, was concerned.

She willed her mind to latch onto any past experience in which she knew she had prayed and God had sustained her, but her thoughts turned and returned to Kelsie. Anne just couldn't shake the nagging feeling that something was really wrong with her daughter and that God wasn't providing any insight.

Cast your cares on the Lord and He will sustain you; He will never let the righteous be shaken. Anne read the card again and shook her head. *Why not try one more trip around the mountain? The outcome might be different this time.* "Lord, I have cast the cares and worries I have for Kelsie onto You. You know what's going on in her, and You know that all I want to do is help her, but I need You to sustain me in this time. I need Your peace that You have her in Your hands, and wisdom as to what to do."

A sudden buzz in her back pocket startled her from her prayer. Brow furrowed and figuring since she had completed the task as best as she could, Anne tugged out her phone and read the text.

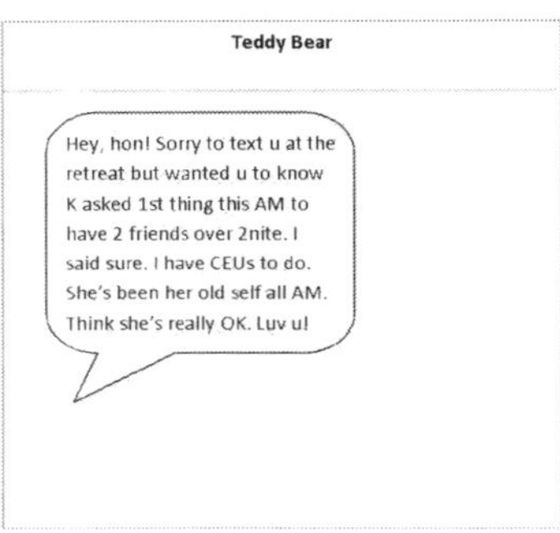

Anne sat stunned. What had changed? Was it because she was gone? Was she doing something wrong? She stared off toward the park, conflicting emotions warring for dominance. Overwhelming thankfulness that Kelsie was her old self dueled with devastating hurt that somehow she had been at fault all along. Her only intention from her daughter's birth was to love and support her in every way possible. So what did this mean? How could she have gotten it so wrong? Anne looked back at the phone, hoping for another text from Ted with more insights, but only his original text glowed back at her.

~~*

At about a quarter to eleven, the ladies had all returned from their practice reflections. Mary noted the faces of each. Some glowed with excitement and satisfaction; others were pensive, as if continuing their reflections, and a few held tear-stained makeup. She was pleased. The range of reactions was exactly as she had hoped. As the ladies settled back into their established seats, she welcomed them back. "It looks like everyone took the assignment to heart and either found some good insights or are working toward them, which is great. We have time for a couple of volunteers to share their experiences before we break for lunch. Don't be shy!"

A nervous chuckle rippled through the attendees, and one brave soul lifted her hand. Mary pointed to her and asked her to stand. "Please tell us your name first."

The striking brunette stood and replied, "I'm Lindsay Davenport. My husband is a private contractor with the military. He travels one weekend a month, but otherwise works out of a naval base near us. Through the years, there have been threats of military cutbacks or the possibilities that certain projects would be transferred, which would mean more time on the road and less at home with our girls. Yet every time word like that comes down from the Pentagon, we pray and put it into the Lord's hands, and He has always been faithful to give us a peace that whatever happens, He's in control."

Tears dampened her voice, but she valiantly continued, "Thus far, we have weathered every possible storm on that front." She cleared her throat and swallowed. One of the ladies sitting beside her gripped her hand in support. Lindsay looked down at her gratefully and then continued, "So, here we have cast our cares and concerns on Him, He has sustained us with the sure knowledge that His will will be accomplished, and we haven't been shaken by any of the possibilities." She looked around at the other ladies and surveyed their reactions like a lawyer who had just finished a moving closing argument. Seeing the nods and smiles, Lindsay sat down.

Mary commented, "That is definitely an example of how that verse has come to pass in your life. Thank you so much, Lindsay, for sharing your story with us." She glanced around the room. "Who's next?"

An older lady toward the back raised her hand, and Mary nodded. "Hi, I'm Genevieve Grady, and my example happened a few years ago. I had a diagnosis of stage two breast cancer, and the Lord sustained me through the diagnosis and treatment, and I'm happy to say I've been cancer-free for three years now."

"How wonderful!" Mary said as a smattering of applause broke out from the group. When the room quieted, she said, "So it sounds like the practice time was very helpful. Before we break for lunch, Jane will be handing out our next verse on a notecard for each of you." She nodded to the pastor's wife, who began to distribute piles of notecards per pew.

Ecclesiastes 3:1

To everything there is a season, a time
for every purpose under heaven.

Mary watched as recognition dawned on the faces, and she saw a few smiles. She waited until each lady had received a card then stated, "We've likely all heard this verse in any variety of circumstances, from deaths to graduations. However, I want you to take the verse and roll it around in your head. View it as if you've never read it before, and reflect on how it holds true for your life. Remember the Five Ws and the H. What have your seasons been? When have seasons started and ended? How did they impact your life?

"This time when you go off to yourself, don't talk to anyone but God. If you get stuck, ask Him to show you your life seasons, and don't just look for the obvious ones: childhood, school, marriage. Look for the little ones: friendships, moments. Don't rush this. Wait to hear the Holy Spirit speak to you."

~~*

While the ladies were recounting their insights from the practice session and Mary continued her teaching, Jane and Kaci snuck outside to set up for the luncheon. Jane had commandeered two of the Seaside security guards to help move the tables and chairs into place, and the Seaside Market had delivered the sandwiches and salads.

The conversations among the group were subdued, which Mary expected, given the nature of the activity. Three ladies had approached her, asking her to expand on a few details about the teaching. Mary had just finished that conversation when a younger lady sidled up.

"Mary? May I ask you a question?" the petite blonde with "Jess" on her nametag asked as she carried the remains of her lunch over to the trash can by the front door.

Mary offered a warm smile and replied, "Of course! Why don't we sit over there?" She gestured to the rock wall that separated the courtyard from the green and opposite the lunch tables filled with other ladies in various stages of eating.

Once they were settled, Jess pursed her lips. Mary waited patiently while Jess collected her thoughts. It was obvious this discussion would be about more than a clarification of the assignment.

"Your story this morning really hit home for me," Jess said as she adjusted her seat on the rock wall. "I've been dating this man, Mitch, for three years, and he's beginning to talk about wanting to get married."

Mary nodded and sensed a caveat coming. She didn't have to wait long.

"But my faith is the most important thing to me while his is—not." Jess paused as if replaying her words, then, embarrassed, quickly added, "I mean, that's not to say he's not a Christian, but his priorities are Alabama football, work, and our relationship. God is barely on the list."

"And you're wondering if that will change after you're married?" Mary prompted.

Jess shook her head. "No, I know it won't. I know the minute we say our vows we'll still be the same people we've always been. We'll just be husband and wife." She stared down at her left hand as if visualizing a wedding band on her fourth finger. After a moment, she cleared her throat and continued, "No, what I've been trying to figure out is, can I be happily married to a man who doesn't have the same spiritual priorities as I do? He gets so uncomfortable when I bring up the topic of faith and want to talk with him about my growth or insights from a sermon. And heaven forbid I tell him about opportunities for himself."

Consternation furrowed her brow and pursed her lips, but she valiantly continued, "He does go to church with me, but only because I think it's important. Like this weekend, he went to tailgate the LSU-Alabama game and planned to stay over through Sunday. His reasoning was that since I wouldn't be there to go to church, he didn't have to go." She shrugged helplessly. "He's a great guy and wants a family, and I do love him, and I know he loves me. So why can't I let go of this need to be on the same spiritual wavelength?"

So this is who God brought to hear my story. Mary smiled with the sympathy of a woman who had walked a similar road, and prayed, *Holy Spirit, give me the words to comfort and to advise.* After a moment of silent contemplation, she said, "As I see it, you have two options. The first is, you could go ahead and marry him and spend however long praying for a change of heart. The second, save yourself the heartache of an unequally yoked marriage and break up with him."

Jess nodded miserably. "Those are exactly the two scenarios that

I've been playing over and over in my mind, but I can't figure out which one is correct."

"Do you hold onto him and pray for his growth, or do you set him free and wait to see if God brings him back to you?" Mary mused. She shook her head, unable to find a response. "I don't have the answer. Either way, you will be relying on God to woo him to a deeper faith. I think the real question is how closely involved is God calling *you* to be in this process?"

She watched as Jess absorbed that question. It was obvious that thought had never occurred to her. After a minute or two, Mary continued, "I think what's the right choice for one couple wouldn't be the right choice for another. For some it would be to marry, trusting that God is working in him to bring him to the fullness of knowing Him. For others it would be to walk away, choosing God over man. Only you know what's right for you."

Jess shot Mary a grateful look and squeezed her hand in thanks. "I appreciate your wisdom. Hopefully by the end of the weekend I'll have an answer one way or another. But most of all, I want peace. I'm tired of living in limbo."

Mary could well imagine. "I'll keep you in my prayers, Jess. And if you need to talk again, just ask."

The younger woman nodded. Seeing the rest of the group had dispersed for the practicum, Mary watched Jess return to the lunch table and gather her things, ready to begin her own reflection. "Lord, be with her," she whispered before returning to her own duties.

Chapter 10

As the rest of the group slipped away, Anne remained seated at the table, still unable to completely process Ted's earlier text. She hadn't had the temerity to text him back with her worries.

The pastor's wife picked up a few stray water bottles and napkins from the lunch area and paused when she reached Anne. Anne started at the kind hand on her shoulder and looked up.

"Are you okay?" Jane asked, concern written in her features.

Unable to form an answer, Anne simply shook her head. Tears welled in her eyes, and Jane quickly pulled out the chair next to her.

"Oh, honey! What's wrong? Is it the reflection work?"

Again, Anne shook her head. "My daughter is thirteen," she began, then stopped midsentence and shook her head again, still unable to comprehend the overnight change in Kelsie. "These past few months, she's been distant and moody and barely says two words to me. I've been really worried that she's depressed, but her teachers and her youth group leaders haven't seen any of the signs of depression."

Anne clasped her hands in her lap, knuckles whitening with the tension. "Then this morning I get a text from my husband saying she asked to have a couple of friends over tonight—something she hasn't done in almost a year—and that she's back to her normal self." She tried to swallow the lump of guilt that had lodged in her throat, but shame wouldn't let it pass. "I'm so sure the problem has to be me, but what do I do? All I ever wanted to do was to be there for her in every way and keep her safe. It's what my mom did for me. But maybe…" She paused as horrified awareness seeped over her. "Am I smothering my daughter?" she whispered.

Anne followed Jane's gaze back toward the chapel. It stood silent, its clapboard exterior gleaming in the late-summer sun. It offered peace and serenity, but no advice for the hurting. That was the role of its people. "Let me tell you something, Anne," Jane began. "I have two grown daughters and now a granddaughter. As moms, they are a part of our hearts and will be, no matter how old they are." Jane turned her gaze back to Anne, eyes filled with wisdom bracketed by lines that spoke of experience. "There were times when each of my girls made decisions that I was really concerned about, but I knew it was their paths they were traveling. Greg and I gave them a good foundation for their faith, and it just got to a point where I had to let go of them. I had to trust that God knew what He had for them to do, and He would protect them." She sighed. "It was one of the hardest things I had to do in my life, but I guess it comes down to who you feel is best able to control life's situations: you or God?"

Anne opened her mouth to protest that of course she trusted that God would take care of Kelsie, but then conviction clenched her heart and closed her lips. Did she really? She knew intellectually that God was always there and could take better care of everything than she ever could, but in reality, Anne wasn't so sure. Maybe that was the real reason she was having such difficulty with the reflection verse.

Jane smiled at Anne's perplexed gaze and patted her shoulder, leaving her to work out her own answer to the question.

~~*

Not in the mood to sit for the assignment, Deli wandered through the park in front of the chapel and meandered between the narrow side streets behind the condos and shops that lined it. Seasons were such an interesting thing to her. As a travel writer, she had profiled areas all over the country as they experienced their changing weather patterns and how from each emerged new opportunities for activity and adventure. They all appeared very definite, not by a particular beginning and ending date—although the calendar did offer its own input—but through signs that helped to determine when one left and the other arrived. In spring, flowers and trees begin to bud. In summer, the sun's rays bake at a hotter temperature. In fall, the leaves change their colors, and winter brings the cooler temperatures and snow. Yet the lines of demarcation for the spiritual seasons of life seemed much more nebulous. These seasons were much more fluid, their beginnings and endings rarely heralded by clear trumpets.

Mary asked us to look deeper to find our seasons, but how, Lord? Deli posed silently. *When I look back on my life, all I can see is the obvious. The day I left for Northwestern. Graduation. The Trib. Going out on my own. What is the deeper revelation? What season am I even in now? Is it beginning or ending?*

Deli came upon a narrow gravel trail that ran between two houses. Curious, she stepped under a whitewashed arbor that boasted a sign with Rose Walk painted in blue lettering. The air cooled several degrees as the scrub oaks' leafy ceiling enclosed her. As she wandered down the trail to the small gazebo, a sense of wonder filled her and a ripple of delight touched her spirit. Perhaps her current season was a both/and, a beginning and an ending?

So, Lord, what is this ending, and what's coming next? Her thoughts drifted back to that morning and the man at the bridge. Certainty that the answer lay there filled her, yet Deli still wondered if the needed courage would meet her somewhere along the path.

Lord, if this is the beginning of the next season, hold my hand and walk me through it, she prayed. *Make me brave.* A thrill skirted through her and bubbled into a giggle. A surge of hope tickled her heart. Deli shook her head in amazed wonder at the Holy Spirit's sudden and comprehensive response. It would seem bravery was on its way.

Ever drawn to gardens for reflection and prayer, Lindsay nestled against the trunk of the old live oak in the middle of the park across from the chapel. Binder in her lap and pen in hand, she leafed through the papers until she reached a blank one, then scrawled the Ecclesiastes verse on the page. Endorphins rushed through her system as her long-defunct analytical skills slowly awakened and her legal mind began to dissect each word. When had she last taken the time to study the Word? She couldn't remember.

Lindsay read her Bible almost every day and took notes during the sermons, but to sit with one verse and pick it apart to determine how it applied to her life? That was new. And new, she found, was exhilarating. She quickly jotted down the obvious seasons in her life, beginning chronologically and ending with the births of her girls. She then paused to do as directed, to consider the deeper and perhaps hidden ones.

With a fond smile, she added Muriel's Bible study and forming friendships with the others to her list. Then she realized it could be argued that the weekend itself was a season.

"Hmmm," she quietly mused as she brushed a couple of oak leaves from her paper. A gentle breeze had risen, and Lindsay watched other loosened leaves drift to the grass. Even though the name "live oak" originated from the trees retaining a majority of their leaves through the fall and winter, it wasn't unusual for a few to brown and fall to make room for new growth.

New growth—trading what is brown for what is green, Lindsay pondered as she studied the leaves. Perhaps it was time for her own new growth, and in order for that to happen, the dead had to fall away. But what was dead in her life? She adored her husband and children, and Fairhope was the most like home of any city she had lived in. Since it wasn't the people and place that were "dead," perhaps it was the situation—specifically her staying at home now that the girls were in school. Maybe her internal struggle was against God tugging her back into the work world. If that were the case though, why would it be so hard to follow?

It was the same question, posed in a different form; yet the answer still seemed to elude her. *Lord, help!* she inwardly cried as she bowed her head.

~~*

Jess had wandered around the courtyard, but she found herself returning to the chapel. Her soul needed whatever connection it could find to this symbol of the faith of her fathers. Although it was a replica rather than genuine, the soothing comfort of the V-groove walls and hardwood floors harkened back to a simpler but harder time on the frontiers of the West, where hardy souls branched into new territory in an effort to make a home for themselves. Many had left family behind, while others had taken the whole clan on the journey. Her ancestors had come from Ireland and headed to Oklahoma for the land rush before a few, weary of battling natives and each other, returned to a more civilized area in Alabama.

A part of her had always wondered what drove them to seek their futures and fortunes in a foreign land. Now a new question joined its ranks: What were their seasons of life? Obviously, they had been children and married and had children. They worked, albeit not in the same manner as she, given the mostly agrarian nature of life back then, but still they labored. Their lives were harder, certainly, but were they intrinsically that much different from her own?

Perhaps it came down to choices and the ability to choose. Women back then could be mail-order brides with no option other than marriage once they arrived at their destinations. They often married for the security of having someone to provide for them and the importance of their intended's faith would have been a luxury. In those cases, Jess guessed, they must have satisfied themselves that the man's overall character was at least of good quality. Either way, each woman would have had to rely on faith that God would protect her and that that had been His plan.

Yet because Jess had the ability and the freedom to choose to begin or end her own season, was she the better or the worse for it? And which season did she choose? Marriage or singlehood? It was most definitely an either/or because she knew for certain that she couldn't continue the current course.

Anne returned to Betty's house after checking in with Jane to confirm there was no session follow-up after the reflection practicum had ended. She pushed open the front door and called to the others as she closed it behind her. A muffled, "Upstairs!" answered her query, and she headed that way.

She found Deli seated on her bed and once more surrounded by Lindsay and Jess. Although there were no tears, there was plenty of emotion pent up in the room. Deli looked indecisive, Jess pensive, and Lindsay on the edge of exasperation. It was the latter who grabbed Anne by the hand and dragged her into the room.

"Just the person! Anne, you have to talk some sense into this girl," Lindsay pleaded as she gestured widely in Deli's direction.

Mystified, Anne answered, "What on earth is going on?"

Deli shook her head and cried, "I don't have anything to wear!" All evidence to the contrary lay strewn across the bed in two haphazard heaps. Anne guessed the largest was the no pile while the smaller was maybe. She ignored the clothing and instead focused on the woman herself.

"You're going paddleboarding, aren't you?" At Deli's nod, she offered, "I would think shorts and a T-shirt would be appropriate."

"But what if I fall off?" Deli proposed. "What happens then? What if my T-shirt is see-through? Which shorts won't show my panties?"

Anne heard Lindsay's exasperated sigh. Apparently they had been around that bend a few times before her arrival. Lindsay's muttered, "I have a thought. What if you don't fall off?" lifted the corners of Anne's lips until she caught the glare Deli sent her way. So, that was obviously a rhetorical question.

Anne picked a few items out of the no pile and with the practical tone of a mother long accustomed to preteen clothing drama, and said, "Well, there's not enough time to have you try on outfits so we can douse you properly." She ignored Jess's snort of amusement and added, "So let's look for darker colors and things that fit a bit looser so you'll be able to move freely if you're above or below water."

Out of the corner of her eye, Anne watched Lindsay swallow her own giggle at the picture she presented, but the greatest impact was on Deli. Notably calmer and possibly more rational, the ebony-haired woman seriously considered her wardrobe until she had narrowed it down to two options. Either was perfectly appropriate in Anne's eyes for the date, but neither she nor the others uttered a word. Deli held up each top in turn in front of the full-length mirror behind her bathroom door as her teeth worried her lower lip. After about five minutes of back and forth, she settled on a neon pink T-shirt and navy shorts. With a pair of silver Sanuk flip-flops, the outfit was complete.

Anne heaved an internal sigh of relief. Crisis averted. Now they just had to make sure she went.

Chapter 11

But Anne needn't have worried on that score. As Deli pedaled her way through WaterColor to the boathouse, she mused that between the afternoon's reflection and Anne's calm practicality, her knee-jerk panic had been soothed. Her concern now rested in how to best to present herself to—with a start, she realized she didn't even know his name.

Houses and trees flew by at a slower pace than the thoughts that now galloped through her head. How was she going to ask about him if he wasn't there? Would anyone know who she was talking about if she did? What if she had misread the invitation? What would—? Deli shook her head and muttered, "No! I am not going to let you run willy-nilly in my head. I am going to trust God and His plan for this evening instead," she said, firmly quelling the negative thoughts that threatened to overwhelm her.

"Wow." She realized with a start that it had been over a decade since she'd had that much difficulty getting her thoughts back under control. "This must be some guy for Satan to be fighting this hard." Deli drew a bit of hope from the revelation and squared her shoulders, perching a bit straighter on the seat of her bicycle.

A few minutes later, she reached the green and a bit of déjà vu skittered through her brain. Although she had been there that morning, there was now a deeper sense of familiarity, as if this meeting had been planned all along. She chuckled and smiled up at the sky, knowing that God was watching with an answering smile of His own. Feeling a tad more confident, she hopped off at the bike rack near the bike barn. A quick spin of the bike lock followed by a quicker prayer for courage, and she was ready.

The object of her journey was leaning against the bridge railing, seemingly in deep contemplation of the trees around him. Deli slowed her approach so as not to startle him. "Hey," she greeted softly.

He turned and loosely unwound from his relaxed pose. "Hey, you made it," he replied with an easy smile. "To be honest, I didn't think you'd come back."

Deli blanched, recalling her earlier reaction, but valiantly walked toward him. Pushing the breath that suddenly clung to her lungs out of the way, she forced herself to ask, "Why not?" and prepared for the critical response she was certain would come.

"Oh, I don't know," he shrugged. "I guess I figured it would be odd for a total stranger to offer to teach a beautiful woman to paddleboard without first introducing himself."

Stunned by him yet again, Deli blinked. *Did he just call me beautiful?* She quickly replayed his comment and found that, sure enough, he had. An amazed chuckle slipped between her lips. "Well, I have to admit that it's not every day that I'm asked if I want to learn to paddleboard," she replied with a grin, her confidence growing.

She stuck out her hand and felt his warm, calloused grip close around it. "I'm—" As her tongue began to form the name she had given in every conversation since grade school, something whispered inside her, *What if God is calling you to step into a new season?* "Delia," she finished. "I'm Delia Preston."

"Delia," he answered as if trying the combination of sounds out in his mouth.

She inwardly shivered. His tongue drew out the E as if it were soaked in sour mash bourbon, sweet and lingering, something to savor. He slowly pumped their joined hands a couple of times and added, "I'm Max Andrews. And it is a pleasure to meet you." He turned, still holding her hand, and tugged her down the incline toward the pier. "I've already got the boards down at the launch. You ready?"

Feeling the warmth of his steady grip seep into her arm, Delia merely smiled and nodded, content to follow him.

"Now, I pulled you a life vest 'cause I didn't know if you could swim. Think you'll need it?"

Delia shook her head. "No, I'm a good swimmer. Not Olympic level, but I won't drown." She spied two paddleboards perched perpendicularly on the pier. One was significantly wider than the other. "What's with the different sizes?"

Max released her hand to grab two paddles, each decorated with an outline of a paddleboarder on one side. "Oh, the larger one is actually a fishing board. Since this is your first time out, I figured you might like to have the extra stability." Seeing her odd look, he quickly added, "But I can get you a regular board, no problem."

He didn't know her from Eve, and yet he cared about her comfort. Amazed at what seemed to be his innate thoughtfulness, Delia grinned and answered, "No, it's perfectly fine."

Pleasure lit Max's eyes, and Delia could feel a corresponding look fill her own. "Okay," he directed. "The first thing to remember is you'll be using your core to paddle, not your arms. So before we get out there, let me show you the most efficient technique."

Delia nodded and watched as he gripped his own paddle with one hand across the T at the top and the other about a third of the way down with his thumb up. "You'll grip the paddle here and here." He nodded to indicate she should try it for herself.

She glanced at each of his hands once more and then mimicked his grips. With eyebrows raised in question, she looked back at him. His approving smile was all the answer she needed.

"Now, you're going to be paddling on both sides of the board in order to stay on course. So every time you need to switch to the other side, you'll need to switch your grips. The opposite hand will always be on top of the paddle." He imitated paddling, changing his grip with each move. He nodded again to Delia for her to try, then reached over to reposition her hand lower on the shaft of the paddle when she changed sides.

"Got it," she said after a minute of trial and error. "What's next?"

He glanced down at the base of the paddle and pointed to the decal. "Always make sure Mr. Paddleboarder is facing forward. He looks ahead, not behind," he added with a cheeky grin.

Delia shook her head in amusement. "Like we should all do, right?"

An appraising light flitted through Max's eyes at her involuntary revelation. "Yeah," he murmured after a moment's consideration. He cleared his throat and turned his gaze to the boards themselves. "Now, you want to always stand in the middle of the board with your feet shoulder-width apart and your knees soft. This will give you the best balance until you get steadier. Ready to give it a shot?"

Delia felt a twinge of nerves, and forcefully reminded herself that she had done scarier things in the name of article writing, but she couldn't remember ever having a more handsome companion. She took in a quick breath and nodded. "Ready as I'll ever be!"

Max eased her board into the water and held it steady near the dock. "The best way to get on is to put your feet in the middle of the board and then kneel. It'll give you time to adjust to balancing on the water. Once you feel secure, you can stand up."

She followed his directions, trusting in his thoroughness, and soon found herself comfortably aboard. "All right, I'm good!"

Max nodded and watched as she slipped a bit further from the dock, easing the paddle into the water and smoothly lifting it out. "You're a natural!" he called as he put his own board into the lake and joined her. "Ready to stand up?"

"I think so. What is the best way so I stay on top of the water?"

"Just do what the turtle said to the hare," he replied, his grin turning boyishly teasing. "Slow and steady. Start with putting one foot under you and begin easing up, and then move the other."

Delia felt his eyes watch her every muscle twitch. Slowly she rose, but still the board wobbled beneath her. "Max!" she cried.

"No worries, Delia, you've got it. Just remember, keep your knees soft. That's going to be the biggest help for balance."

Delia bent her knees a bit and felt the board steady beneath her. With a sigh of relief, she put the paddle back in the water and, remembering his instruction on altering her grips, began to paddle.

"That's it! You're golden," he cheered.

She turned to flash him a triumphant grin, and the board wobbled beneath her. "Oh no!" Taking in a calming breath, she leaned forward just a tad and once again found her center of gravity. "You said this is a fishing paddleboard? How in the world could anyone fish off this? I would end up in the drink with my catch!" She could feel the wattage of Max's grin gain intensity. "Okay, obviously I'm not ready to look over my shoulder, so that means you need to get up here where we can safely talk!"

Max quickly obliged, and soon they were paddling away from the boathouse. A few minutes later, he asked, "So, have you ever been to this area?"

Delia cautiously shook her head. "No, this the first for me. Although I'm actually surprised since I'm a travel writer by trade, and this seems like it would be a vacationer's haven. Based on what you've said and your skill on a board, I'm guessing that wouldn't be you, though. So that leaves either a local or a homeowner who gets down here frequently."

Impressed by her insight, Max answered, "It's actually the latter, but I would love if it were the former." He turned and pointed behind him. "I own a house that backs up to the north side of Western Lake. You can just see it through the trees over there."

Delia shook her head and replied, "Thanks, but I'll take your word for it!"

He grinned and continued to talk, his words accented by the soothing sounds of water hitting their paddles. "My family has owned a sawmill in South Carolina going back to my great-grandfather. When my dad died five years ago, the day-to-day operations fell to me. I travel occasionally for meetings with our bigger clients and of course for the annual meeting, which is why I'm here now."

Delia absorbed his words and the sounds of the breeze as it lifted the pine needles and waved the grasses. The silence that fell between them was oddly comforting. Much to her surprise, there was no rush of nerves urging her to break it. Max seemed equally at peace, content to take in the scenery, while still occasionally checking on her efforts. Yet even though she enjoyed the tranquil peace that enveloped them, her journalistic instincts soon began to bubble up until she could no longer keep the questions at bay. "So, since you're in timber and practically a local, I'm guessing you could tell me about the area. How has it stayed so undeveloped? I'm surprised there aren't houses all over this lake, as beautiful as it is."

"And I'm sure there would be if that weren't protected land on the west and northwest side," Max said as he steered them up toward the first northern bend of the lake. He gestured widely with his paddle at the expanse before them. "The state of Florida has always owned much of the land down here, with the St. Joe Company falling in second place. Everything behind us is St. Joe—beginning here and moving west is the eastern side of Grayton Beach State Park, which was created in '67. Miles of trails loop around in there, and on the Gulf side there's a full RV park."

She soaked up his words with a different intention than ever before in her career. While his enthusiasm and warmth were evidence of his deep love for the area and similar to what others she had interviewed possessed, this was not information to remember for an article. Rather, something inside her yearned to know him better, encouraging her to continue peppering him with questions as they paddled.

A few minutes later, Max paused their perambulation and discussion of the area wildlife. "Now, one more thing to know about maneuvering on a board is how to turn." Delia listened to his quiet teacher tones and followed his instructions for making a C turn, readily changing her paddle's direction. "We have two options at this point," he said. "We can paddle under 30A and head to the southern portion of the lake or continue up the northern arm. You're going to really need to watch your balance under the bridge, but we can go whichever way you'd like."

She paused as they began to make the curve and looked in the direction of the road as it spanned the dune lake. The short gap from the water to the bridge was surprising, but the scene that gaped her mouth was the tree line beyond it. A canopy of pines trailed toward the dunes on the Gulf side of the lake, towering soldiers taking a final stand against the shoreline and Gulf beyond. "Oh, wow! That's gorgeous!"

Max agreed. "That stand of pines is one of the trademarks of 30A. You'll find it on everything from T-shirts to paintings and even bottles of wine."

"I can see why," Delia said, marveling.

Opting for the northern arm, they paddled a little further, returning to that oddly comfortable silence. A little while later, Delia's flagging energy and the sun's lowering profile made her glad to see the pier up ahead. Once there, Max hopped off his board and onto the deck with a grace that spoke of comfort and long practice. Delia laughed at his instinctive showboating and denied any desire to try the move for her own dismount. "No, thank you, sir! I'll stick to the traditional method."

Max shot her a disappointed look, but any hint of ill will was removed by his teasing grin. "All right, traditional it is. Scoot over till you're butted up against the dock for the length of the board, then kneel back down." He watched as she tried to determine where to place the paddle, then said, "Here, I'll take that." Laying it aside, he continued, "Now, you'll do the opposite of what you did when you got on board. You'll ease up until you can scoot your bottom onto the deck."

Delia did as she was instructed and soon was back on dry land. Or at least closer to it. She watched Max slide each board out of the water then looked up at him. She started to grin, delight mixed with relief that both she and her clothes were still dry. However, his serious gaze stalled the lifting of her lips. She opened her mouth to ask what was wrong, but before she could form the words, he took her hand and helped her to stand. "I've got a dinner I have to attend tonight, but can I see you tomorrow?"

Delia was floored by the question and the sincerity in his gaze. Not trusting her own eyes, she blinked. He was still there, as was his question. "I'm here for a church retreat with some friends. We're studying reflection and meditation, and I'm not sure when it will be over." She was babbling, but she couldn't help herself.

Max grinned at her and raised a finger to her lips to silence the verbal stream. He asked again, "So, can I see you tomorrow?"

This time her lips did lift in response. As she nodded, his finger gently rubbed against her them, igniting the most pleasant sensation of warmth.

Apparently now aware of his finger's location, Max quickly lowered his hand and cleared his throat, embarrassment tingeing his cheeks. "How about a walk on the beach and then dinner?"

"That sounds perfect."

"I'll meet you at the beach access in Seaside, then. Say five o'clock?"

"Five o'clock," she answered before turning to go. "And Max? Thank you for today. I had a wonderful time."

Pleasure warmed his eyes and his smile. "So did I."

~~*

The crunch on the gravel driveway heralding the return of a bicycle had Lindsay glancing at the large wall clock in the living room. Six forty-five. Almost three hours. She mentally crossed her fingers that all was well.

The three had spent a quiet evening nibbling on their prepurchased sandwiches and wraps. Jess had been correct in her estimation that they would be reluctant to face the hustle and bustle of a popular restaurant in their postreflection states. Instead they each nestled into a different nook of the downstairs, Lindsay content to text with John while Anne and Jess quietly read on their iPads.

The front door opened, revealing Deli. Like earlier that morning, she closed the door behind her and leaned back against it with a dazed look on her face. But this time, Lindsay could feel the joy radiating off her. With an expectant smile that was mirrored by Anne and Jess, she asked, "Well? How did it go?"

Deli smiled, disbelief warring with joy. "Um, wow. Just…yeah… wow." She nodded slowly then pushed herself off the door and headed upstairs.

Lindsay shared a grin with Jess and Anne before they quietly chorused, "Yes!"

Chapter 12

Anne awoke to the ding from her phone signaling a new text message. She had slept fitfully in spite of the talk with Jane, her thoughts returning home no matter how hard she tried to center them. Kelsie was having her sleepover. It was the first she had initiated in a year, and Anne wasn't there to make cookies or help pick out clothes for dress-up or choose songs for an impromptu dance party. While she had prayed it was a huge success, she couldn't help but focus on how conveniently it had coincided with her absence. It was almost a slap in the face, awakening her to a reality that she had somehow played a role in Kelsie's behavior of late. Guilt attacked, quickly and effectively, tossing and turning her even in sleep, its lashing sting finding all her vulnerabilities with unerring accuracy.

Awaiting the final nail in her coffin, she leaned across the bed, unplugged the phone, and settled herself on the edge of the mattress to read the text.

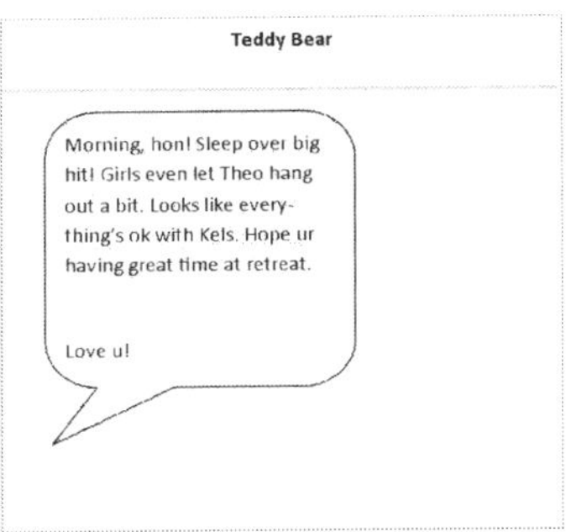

So, it is true, Anne thought. Her worst fears were confirmed. She was the reason behind Kelsie's moodiness and silence. She fell back on the bed, tears streaming from her eyes, then read the message again. Knowing Ted would be expecting some sort of reply given the early hour, she thumbed over to the emoticons and sent him a thumbs-up. It wasn't a reflection of her current emotional state, but it was the best she could do without worrying him.

"Oh, God, help!" she cried as she tossed the phone on the bed. "What in the world do I do?"

Hearing the creak of the floorboard in the hall and knowing the others would be up, Anne wiped her eyes and pulled herself together. She couldn't collapse. There was the retreat to get through, and Lindsay and Jess were dealing with issues of their own. Besides, there wasn't anything she could do about her relationship with Kelsie from two hundred miles away.

~~*

"For many Christians, the word *meditation* is scary because it brings to mind all sorts of New Age connotations, but in fact the opposite is true," Mary said. This was always the section of the seminar that tended to have the most people wiggling in their seats, as paradigms and preconceived notions were triggered and reframed or shattered altogether. Today, though, there seemed to be little wiggling and a refreshing amount of mostly confident, ready gazes staring back at her.

"There are actually twenty different instances in the Bible where we are specifically directed to meditate. However, the biggest distinguishing factor between Christian and New Age meditation is the topic. New Age meditation incorporates the universe, nature, the inherent goodness of man, etc. In Christian meditation, we meditate on the Word, for it is the basis for our faith and the only source of truth. Man is not inherently good and needs a Savior.

"So when we talk about meditation from the scriptural perspective, we need to first consider what God intended for the practice. Two words are primarily used in the Old Testament from which our English word *meditation* is translated. They are *haga* and *sihach.* The first means to ponder, groan, or meditate. The second means to contemplate, muse, or rehearse over and over in one's mind. Given that second definition, can anyone think of another English word with a less positive connation?

Mary waited and, when no hands were raised, she prompted, "Think of the last time you had a big holiday party at your house. How many of you contemplated how everyone would get along, mused over whether everyone would like the food, or rehearsed over and over what you would say to your mother-in-law when she arrived?" A handful of giggles and more than a few smiles answered Mary's question. "I'm sure every one of you now knows what word I'm talking about, right? *Worry.* So given the comparable definitions for *worry* and *meditation,* as Rick Warren has said, 'If you can worry, you can meditate!'"

With a compassionate smile to offset the stern statement, she continued, "Now that we've established that meditation should be second nature to most of us, what are the different ways we can meditate? There are several types of meditation that may be done. One ancient practice from the monasteries is that of *lectio divina.* In this style, a passage of Scripture is first read deliberately, often slowly or in different postures, such as standing, kneeling, or sitting. Once the passage has been read, it is then pondered. Specific questions should be asked and answered about the text. The third step is a dialog with God about the reading, asking Him to reveal the truth of the Scripture. Finally, one rests with God in His presence, basking in the revelation.

"I personally enjoy *lectio divina,* but for those just beginning the practice of meditation, it can be a bit daunting, so I've developed a simpler way to come to a similar result. Jane will hand out the notes for each of you to follow along with." Mary waited for Jane to distribute the material before continuing.

Meditation 101

1. Read the verse.
2. What is God saying?
3. Do a word study.
4. What is God saying?
5. Read the verse with the new or expanded knowledge from the word study.
6. What is God saying?
7. What is God saying to me?

Once each lady received the handout, Mary continued. "Obviously, we are going to start with reading the verse. But it's the way the verse is read that is important. Don't merely run through it, especially if it's a verse that you have read previously or even memorized. Take your time. Read it slowly, and absorb each word. You might even choose a different translation of the Bible to offset your familiarity with the verse.

"Next, ask, 'What is God saying in this verse?' This is to get a general understanding of the message that's being presented. If you want, you may read the verse in context by going back a couple of verses and forward a couple. Often, the meaning is enhanced by the context.

"The following step is where we dig in. The Word of God should be looked at like a fine wine. There are many undertones and nuances that are missed if the sip is not taken slowly and savored so that each flavor—or, in this case, meaning—can be determined and appreciated. As such, we will embark on a word study of key words in the verse. When you return home, I would encourage each of you to pick up a *Strong's Concordance* and *Vine's Expository Dictionary* for your personal study. For practicality's sake, though, I have already picked out and defined the words from the verses you will receive for your meditation practicum. Jane will distribute the definition packets in a few minutes.

"Before you go back to the verse now that you have the definitions, we'll need to ask what God is saying in those target words individually? Once you have a handle on that, we'll use those definitions and the Lord's revelation of them, and put them back into the verse. The verse should now come alive even more with the added knowledge and detail that the word study and insight have provided.

"Again, you'll ask, 'What is God saying?' followed by the question 'What is God saying to me personally?' Other questions you might find yourself asking are 'Why is God showing me this verse?' and 'What does He want me to either see or learn?' The most interesting thing about this type of study is that often you will receive continued insight or revelation several days after you first complete the study. Your spirit will roll everything around in your brain over the following days to allow you time to fully process the verse and its impact on you. So if you don't receive immediate enlightenment during the study, don't be concerned. Simply wait. God is patient and wants you to receive the full revelatory knowledge of Him.

"How is everyone doing?" Mary asked as she scanned the group. "Any questions or concerns?" When no one raised a hand, she smiled and said, "All right, let's get to it! As I said previously, I asked the Holy Spirit to help me hand-select verses for this weekend that would be beneficial to each attendee. Now, I'm not prophetic enough to look at each of you and hand out a specific verse." She paused as a chuckle rippled through the group. "But I am confident that the Holy Spirit can and will provide a verse that is spot-on for the road each of you are traveling."

She turned and picked up a black velvet bag from the chair behind her and made a show of shaking it up. "We are going to follow the time-honored tradition of drawing. Each lady will draw out one card. The verse will be on one side, and the other side will be blank. Jane will distribute the word study definition lists separately after lunch, and we'll break for the meditation practicum at that time." Mary bowed her head and closed her eyes to pray over the bag of verses. "Lord, give the truth of your word to each woman here as she needs it. Open each eye and ear to the fullness of your meaning. Amen. Now, I'd like each of you to come up one at a time, rather like communion, and select your verse."

Kaci returned to the music stand while the attendees stood and began to form two lines. She fastened her guitar strap around her neck and quietly strummed Leeland's "Christ Be All Around Me" as Mary gestured for the ladies to approach. A few minutes later, when each had received her verse and returned to her pew, Kaci invited them to stand and sing.

~~*

Jess beckoned to Lindsay as she grabbed her boxed lunch, a bottle of water, and a napkin from the main table and sidled between two other tables to reach her friends. Anne sat, absently chewing her shrimp salad wrap, her mind likely two hundred miles away. Ted had texted her that morning that the sleepover had been a huge hit, which had thrown Anne for an even curvier loop. Deli was equally distant, although hers was a considerably shorter distance of perhaps two miles. She hadn't drifted off her perch on cloud nine since she had returned from her date the night before and had to be practically pinched to turn her attention to breakfast earlier that morning. That left Lindsay and Jess to start and maintain any luncheon conversation.

The brunette shook her head and let out a sigh as she pulled out the chair and plopped down across from Jess. "I don't know, Jess, but I think the Holy Spirit may have gotten my verse wrong. Either that or I need to trade with someone."

Jess paused midbite to judge if Lindsay was being facetious. Seeing the frustration carved into her friend's brow, she decided that Lindsay wasn't in a joking mood. "Why do you think that?" she asked as she lowered her wrap.

Lindsay shrugged and pried open her box to reveal her requested lettuce wrap and picked up a half. Waving it toward Jess to accent her point, she said, "Mine is all about fear, and I can't think of a single thing that I'm afraid of that's impacting me right now. Sure, I'm waffling about going back to work, but that's more about concern for my girls and how it would impact them."

Jess opened her mouth to suggest that concern was considered an offshoot of fear, but instead took a bite of her own wrap when she saw that Lindsay's nonjoking mood also didn't extend to a discussion of facts. It appeared she had a full head of steam and was prepared to barrel through any argument that ran contrary to what she had already determined. It was no wonder she had been such a successful attorney.

Lindsay finally decided to eat her lunch rather than conduct an orchestra with it and munched quietly for a moment. Jess was fairly certain the topic hadn't died, but she decided not to wave a red flag in front of her friend. Instead she glanced over at Deli, who had barely picked at her food, preferring to stare off in the direction of the boathouse. Jess jostled her elbow. When that didn't bring her back, Jess called, "Dehlleee?" and waved her hand in front of her friend's face. Still she didn't move. "Del?" she asked again, then finally forcefully added, "Delia!"

Delia jumped, then glanced sheepishly over at Jess. "You okay?" Jess asked with a teasing grin.

Delia nodded. “Sorry,” she answered, and then *sotto voce*, “he called me Delia. And for the first time in my life, it felt right.”

Jess’s smiled brightened. “Oh, I’m so glad!” she beamed. After a moment’s thought, she asked, “Should we call you Delia?”

A considering light flashed through Delia’s eyes. Her brow wrinkled as she mulled over the question, feeling it out for correctness. A moment later, she nodded. “Yeah, I think I’d like that.”

Jess nodded and reached over to squeeze her friend’s hand. “Me, too,” she replied.

“So what were y’all’s verses?” Lindsay asked, having missed the byplay between Jess and Delia. “Maybe we could trade.”

Delia shook her head. “No taker here. Mine is completely on target.”

Jess agreed. “Mine is exactly what I needed to hear. You know, Mary did say that sometimes you don’t get the insight right away with a meditation. Why don’t you give your verse a shot, Lindsay, and see if something doesn’t hit you later?”

Lindsay chewed on that option for a moment, then nodded. “Good point. If nothing else, it can be practice for meditation.”

Behind them, Jane tapped on a silver triangle to gain the group’s attention. “Ladies, if you’ll begin to finish up your lunches, I have your word study definitions ready for you to get started on the meditation practicum.”

Lindsay crumpled her napkin and tossed it in the box with the remains of her wrap. “Okay, let’s get this party started.”

Jess winced at her friend’s obvious impatience and sent a prayer heavenward for peace and revelation. After a quick review, she added her own name to that request. She could use some peace and revelation, too.

~~*

Lindsay tapped her verse index card against her thigh as she paced the length of the chapel aisle, unable to settle on a specific place for her meditation practicum. *What is wrong with me?* The reflection verse had been perfectly fine, and she had been able to gain some good insights during that portion of the retreat. What happened? But she knew the answer. It was the verse that Mary said the Holy Spirit had given her:

> Do not fear, for I am with you; do not be <u>afraid</u>, for I am your God. I will <u>strengthen</u> you; I will help you; I will hold on to you with My <u>righteous</u> right hand.
>
> Isaiah 41:10

Do not fear. Do not be afraid. She was neither. Of course she was facing a difficult decision and she was cognizant of the possible outcomes. She also wanted to make the best decision for her family. But, she was absolutely, positively certain she wasn't afraid. After all, if she were afraid, then she would be disappointing her father. Again.

A sob suddenly wracked her body, and Lindsay stuffed a fist in her mouth to quiet the unthinking wail. She scrabbled for the end of a pew, the fear finally given voice, and she collapsed under the years of her self-imposed silence. *Oh, God.* She was afraid. No, she was more than afraid. She was terrified.

What if she made the wrong decision? What if she selfishly chose to put herself first when God had another path for her? It had worked out the first time, but the price had been almost too high. Her mind flitted back to the only time she had knowingly chosen for herself and hugely disappointed her father. No, she wasn't going to go there. She wasn't going to feel that pain again. She was not. But, as the memory coalesced into full-on HD color and sound, it appeared the Holy Spirit had other plans.

It was the hardest thing Lindsay had done in her life: telling her proud father that she wouldn't be majoring in engineering. It had been his heart's desire that she would follow in his footsteps. Since he hadn't had a son, Robert Duncan had poured his knowledge and appreciation of chemical processes into his daughter. Lindsay, craving the love and affection of the emotionally distant man, had soaked up every topic. When high school graduation came, and with it her guaranteed acceptance into Georgia Institute of Technology, she had been ready to take up the gauntlet.

But one fateful meeting with the guidance counselor regarding her aptitude test results up-ended all of her father's well-laid plans. Lindsay had certainly scored high in the logic and rational sections, but her aptitudes lay outside the realm of science and math. To her surprise, she had ranked higher in societal and ethical concerns. Lindsay had explained her plans and acceptance into GIT, but the kindly older woman encouraged her to seriously consider what her test results showed.

It had taken a week of agonizing and further study before her heart finally overruled what had been drilled into her head for years. When she broached the topic with her parents, her mother had been supportive of whatever she decided, affirming that it was her decision to make. Her father had gone silent and remained that way throughout her well-planned speech. As soon as she finished her reasons and desires, he looked away with a shrug and muttered, "It's your life. I suppose you can mess it up any way you choose. I'll be interested to see how long this lasts."

Reading the shock on Lindsay's face, her mother had forced him to apologize, but the damage had been done. Lindsay spent her undergraduate years at Emory, proving him wrong: president's list every semester, scoring a 178 on her LSAT, being accepted into Emory's law school, and finally being awarded one of the prestigious scholarships in the Woodruff Scholars Program.

As she moved up each year, her father watched her flourish and grudgingly came to accept the rightness of her choice. Yet neither his acceptance nor meeting the love of her life tempered the stab of guilt that circumvented her rationalizations and continued to prick her soul. She had still greatly disappointed the most important man in her life at the time.

Chapter 13

When the ladies were released to begin their meditation practicum, Jess left the churchyard and headed back to the house to the porch's oversized bed swing. Feeling the need to be tucked away from everyone as her heart pondered the only question she had, she snuggled into the deep cushions and crossed her legs Indian style. Her sandals lay askew on the deck, and on the swing's arm, the plastic tumbler of tea beaded up with the auspicious beginnings of a well-formed sweat ring. The sheer curtains that hung in the corners of the porch ready to be pulled for privacy swayed as the light breeze touched them. Above her, the ceiling fan beat a lazy tempo. All was peace. Well, all but her insides.

The weekend had turned bittersweet. It had been sweet to see the beginning of Delia's relationship and to relish with her good friend in the blessings of a burgeoning love, and yet bitter as all the questions in Jess's spirit were slowly being nudged toward confirmation. It was time to release Mitch.

Yet even as her heart broke at the thought, she wondered if she hadn't seen the signs of that end all along. Was it a relationship God would permit? Certainly. Was it His best? Jess wasn't so sure. She had prayed for Mitch and their relationship often throughout the last three years. Her words had been strong, sure, and based on His Word, but even then something always gave her pause.

Jess had learned early on that God wants His children equally yoked so there is no striving between them. It was His design for the man to be the spiritual head of the household. As she grew in age and faith, she realized the importance of that role more fully. Her father had abdicated that position in her own family, and even though her mother capably took up the reins of her Christian education, there always seemed to be a hole in their home.

Although she and Mitch had a mostly harmonious relationship, no matter how often or sincerely she prayed, there remained a lingering certainty that he would follow in her father's footsteps, leaving her to walk in her mother's. That was the last thing Jess wanted for her marriage. Sadly, her refusal to prolong her family legacy kept butting up against Mitch's apathy.

> "Peace I leave with you, My <u>peace</u> I give to you; not as the world gives do I give to you. Let not your heart be <u>troubled</u>, neither let it be <u>afraid</u>."
>
> John 14:27

Jess sighed, once more at an impasse. She pulled the verse index card out and began to read, "'Peace I leave with you, My peace I give to you; not as the world gives do I give to you. Let not your heart be troubled, neither let it be afraid.' Oh, Lord, peace is what I have been praying for all this time. Peace to know if I should marry Mitch…or peace to let him go. I haven't found either, and I'm so tired of living in this limbo." She paused as she considered the words before her. "But here You say You have already given us your peace. So if it's already available, where do I find it?"

She leaned her head back against the pillow and stared at the aqua ceiling, painted that color to draw the mosquitoes up and away from the occupants of the porch, although Jess figured the screens encompassing the porch deterred the insects much more effectively. The lazy wobble of the fan blades rotated steadily accented by the regular click of the fan motor. She could stay there all day, basking in the soothing surrounds. She could, but that would provide only a temporary balm to her turmoil.

With a grumbling sigh, she pulled the binder to her lap and flipped to the meditation practicum questions. A quick reread of the directions told her she had inadvertently completed the first two tasks, so she moved on to the word study. Mary had underlined *peace*, *troubled*, and *afraid* for Jess to research. The word choices were eerily on target.

The first was something she desperately longed for and the latter two aptly described her current emotional state. "Lord, please give me some answers," she prayed as she read through the word list alphabetically.

"Afraid, from the Greek word *deilos*, meaning timid." She tugged the chapel pen out of the binder's front pocket and circled the word *timid*. "Hmm. Well, that's still a good descriptor of what I'm feeling because I really don't want to confront Mitch on this when I already know where he stands."

She flipped back a few pages and found *troubled*. "The Greek word is *tarasso*, meaning agitated. That also fits." She sighed and once again circled the definition. "Now for some *peace*," she murmured with a wry smile. "*Eirene*, a sense of rest and contentment." She breathed, "Oh, yes, Lord. Send that my way."

Having found each of the definitions, Jess pulled the index card back to the front and compared the three words to the definitions in the context of the verse. "Peace, a sense of rest and contentment, I leave with you, My peace, a sense of rest and contentment, I give to you; not as the world gives do I give to you. Let not your heart be troubled, or agitated, neither let it be afraid or timid."

Jess lifted her tumbler out of the pooling sweat ring as she mulled over the new information. She swallowed a mouthful of the tea and leaned back once more against the pillows. "What are You saying in this verse, Lord? What are You trying to tell me?" she murmured. "You say You have already given me Your peace. So why don't I feel it?" She fell silent, contemplating her questions and waiting for answers.

A few beats of the fan blades later, she mused, "Peace was given, like a gift, right? So like a gift…" She trailed off as awareness gently seeped into her heart. "Something can be given, but it also has to be accepted. A gift is a gift, yes…but if you don't choose to accept it…it remains unopened." A slow smile crept across her lips. "So if You've already given me peace, I just have to accept that I have Your peace." Relief flooded her. It had been there all along. The peace and the answer. "Thank you, Lord," she whispered.

~~*

Delia settled on a bench in the little park across from the WaterColor tennis courts and faced an access point to the Western Lake trail. She had skimmed her verse after she had drawn it from the bag, and her confidence had surged. Unfortunately, the break for lunch had given her thoughts enough time to tumble and twist into a confusing mix of possibilities and promises. All of which centered on Max and their dinner date that night.

What if she had misread not only Max's intent, but also God's word for her? *Mary said that we were to look for a deeper meaning beyond the obvious.* Delia pursed her lips at the thought. She studied the index card again.

> "Look, I am about to do something new; even now it is coming. Do you not see it? Indeed, I will make a way in the wilderness, rivers in the desert."
>
> Isaiah 43:19

While the obvious comforted, it was entirely possible that the deeper would caution. She paused at the realization, but then her writer's curiosity got the better of her. Even with that risk, she couldn't pass up the opportunity to find out.

A quick review of the directions, and she was ready to begin. What was God saying? The most obvious was that He was going to do something different from what was currently happening. He wanted the reader to be aware of what He was planning and even gave two examples of what would occur. She flipped to a blank sheet of paper in her binder and jotted the number two down, making a few notes of her insights next to it.

After adding a number three below them, she pulled out the packet of papers that served as an abridged dictionary and began to sift through the entries. She decided to take each word as it came in the verse rather than going alphabetically. "New, coming, way, desert," Delia murmured as she added each to her list.

2) do something different; not been done before; two examples: path and rivers

3)
New
Hebrew: *chadash* "khaw-dawsh"
Def: new or renewed; recent or fresh but also not previously existing

Coming:
Hebrew: *tsamach* "tsaw-makh"
Def: sprouting, springing forth, bud forth

Way
Hebrew: *derek* "deh-rek"
Def: a road, course of life, or mode of action

Desert
Hebrew: *yshiymown* "yesh-ee-mone"
Def: desolation, solitary

Now, what is God saying with these words? she pondered. *What He is doing will be fresh or will have happened recently. It's happening quickly because* sprouting, springing, and budding *indicate speed. It's not a slow progression, given the words are active verbs rather than passive. The new way is a course of life or mode of action that will be created.*

She wasn't surprised by the definitions of the first three target words, but the last, *desert*, did give her pause. "Solitary," she murmured. "Really?" It made sense when one thought about it because it was very easy to feel alone in a desert, but usually there were caravans that traipsed their way through, providing plenty of company. Yet, in this verse, God was saying that this new way of life wouldn't be solitary.

Stunned, Delia dropped her pen and stared blankly at the notes in her lap. Unable to fully comprehend what she thought she had read, she pulled the index card with her verse back out and held it above her definition list then proceeded to read it once more, her voice trembling with cautious expectation. "Look, I am about to do something new, recent, fresh and not previously existing; even now it is coming, sprouting, springing forth, budding forth. Do you not see it? Indeed, I will make a way, a road, course of life, mode of action in the wilderness, rivers in the desert, desolation, solitary."

She paused, then read it again, using the definitions in place of the original words. "Look, I am about to do something not previously existing; even now it is springing forth. Do you not see it? Indeed, I will make a course of life in the wilderness, rivers in the solitary." A surge of hope shot through her system. Exhilaration caught its coattails and zinged along her nerve endings. Max. That feeling of déjà vu wasn't just her imagination. Their meeting had been preordained.

Delia sucked in a steadying breath and gripped the edge of the bench in a vain effort to steady herself. This was not the panic of previous occasions, rather it was the breathtaking sensation of pure joy. As she began to slow her rapid breathing, Delia found that pure joy could be just as earth-shattering as full-on panic.

Oh. My.

~~*

Unlike the others who sought solitude for their practicum, Anne craved life. The bustling atmosphere of Seaside provided plenty of it. After wandering down the cobbled streets, dodging bicyclists and running children let loose from school on fall break, she finally settled at the tables outside the Seaside Market. She had splurged on one of the market's famous private-label sodas, opting for the black cherry, then had staked out a table under the awning where she could ponder and people-watch.

Sparrows hopped around her feet, ever optimistic of the fall of table scraps. She shook her head at them. "Sorry, little guys, no food here. Best be on your way." She glanced over at a young couple with a toddler as they opted for a table closer to the street, then encouraged her feathered companions, "Now, the table over there looks promising!" As they hopped away, intent on their search, Anne studied her index card.

> Now this is the <u>confidence</u> that we have in Him that if we ask <u>anything</u> according to His <u>will</u>, He <u>hears</u> us.
>
> 1 John 5:14

Mary's verse for her was all about prayer. Anne had been doing quite a bit of that over the last few months as Kelsie became slightly more irritable and infinitely more silent, and Anne was quickly tiring of praying, of lifting up, of believing and not seeing. She pursed her lips. How much longer did she have to pray? There were times when she felt like the widow who badgered the king over and over, but all her entreaties seemingly fell on deaf ears.

Yet there were other times, like when she had prayed for her sister-in-law to find a job, that they seemed to skyrocket right to the head of the list and were answered immediately. Not that she didn't love Ted's sister, but it would have been considerably more satisfying if her answered prayer had been for Kelsie.

Anne read through the verse again, this time noting the words Mary had chosen for the word study, and her mind caught on *will*. She knew that one had to pray God's will for the requests to be answered, but since that was the case, why hadn't her prayer for Kelsie been answered? Anne's only motivation was wanting the best for her daughter. *And wouldn't that be in God's will? For that matter, shouldn't a harmonious household where the child honors the parents be right in the center of God's will, given He had carved that admonition into one of two stone tablets thousands of years ago?*

She sighed and watched the young family for a moment, the toddler happily jettisoning large pieces from his muffin onto the ground, much to the delight of the sparrows. His mother was not amused and moved the muffin out of reach. His wail of frustration returned her hand to the treat, and she began tearing small bites off for him to eat, mollifying him for the moment.

Reluctant to return to the meditation practicum, Anne turned her attention to an older gentleman walking behind a fluffy Bichon Frise. He paused at the small dish of water outside the market's doors while the dog lapped gleefully. She smiled and watched them meander on their way a moment later.

Anne forcefully shook her head. She was stalling, and she knew it. Frowning at a flicker of guilt, she reminded herself that she had been the one to promote the weekend to the others, and she had definitely felt confirmation in her spirit that it was the right place to be. So these distractions were obviously the enemy's way of keeping her from learning what she needed to learn.

She had to admit he definitely knew what he was doing by taunting her with her chosen verse. To her, it looked like she was about to take yet another trip around the same mountain. Praying. Asking. Seeking. And no revelation. However, Mary said she had relied on the Holy Spirit's direction for selecting the verses, and Anne had to trust that there was method behind the seeming madness in her choice. She sighed and, with resignation slowing her hand, began to flip through the word study definition list.

"Confidence," she muttered. "*Parrhesia*, absence of fear, cheerful courage, boldness. *Well, if there's one thing I am not in my prayers,* she thought with a sigh, *it is cheerfully courageous.* "Anything, any person or object." *At least that's helpful. Kelsie must be in there somewhere then.* "And finally, *will, thelema*, of one's will, choice, inclination, desire, pleasure. Hmmm."

Anne dropped the packet of paper to the table and slumped in the metal chair. "God, what are You saying? Is the reason my prayer hasn't been answered because it's not Your desire or inclination? Or worse, do I already have Your revelation that I have been the problem all along? If either is true, where do I go from here? Kelsie seems much happier with me gone, but I can't leave Ted and Theo just to keep her happy. That would destroy me and them. Then where would we be? I have only wanted the best for Kelsie, like my mom did for me. What about that is so wrong?"

Anger and frustration bubbled within her buffeting her already confused and fatigued heart. Anne felt justified in each emotion, but she also knew there was still one question left to ask: what was the truth?

She mentally put a fist around each troubling issue, collecting them all together to ponder. She inhaled deeply then slowly released the breath, calm and perspective returning. Was breaking up a household God's will? No. Was ignoring prayers in God's nature? No. Did God say things and not follow through? No.

A relieved sigh escaped her lips as the last vestiges of the anger and frustration slipped away. The truth was, God did answer prayers. He did mean His Word. His will was to heal her relationship with Kelsie. The actual question, then, was how did He want to do that?

~~*

Unable to answer the unanswerable at that point and unwilling to stew in the negative thoughts Satan was throwing her way, Anne gathered her items and headed back toward the chapel, ready to meet up with any of the other ladies and discuss their dinner plans.

She found Lindsay seated in a pew about halfway down the chapel's aisle. Quietly approaching in case her friend was in deep contemplation, she slid into the pew next to her and began to soak up the peace found in the four walls. Anne glanced over a few minutes later to find Lindsay, tear-stained cheeks still damp, gazing up at the cross.

Alarmed, Anne whispered, "Lindsay, are you okay?"

Lindsay sighed and shook her head. "No, not really. That verse really rocked me." She reached over and clenched Anne's hand, seeking support and comfort, then slid her notecard over for Anne to read.

> Do not fear, for I am with you; do not be <u>afraid</u>, for I am your God. I will <u>strengthen</u> you; I will <u>help</u> you; I will hold on to you with My <u>righteous</u> right hand.
>
> Isaiah 41:10

"I have been fighting fear for most of my life," Lindsay whispered, "but this is the first time I have ever been called on it so directly."

"Oh, honey!" Anne cried as she pulled Lindsay into a side hug.

"Was that what you meant when you told Deli about triggering the other day?"

Lindsay nodded sadly, shame stealing over her cheeks. She ducked her head away from Anne's too perceptive gaze. "My father was so disappointed when I told him I was going to major in law rather than engineering. I had never let him down before, and he made it plainly known that I had." She paused and swallowed hard. "So I spent all of my school years and most of my career trying to prove to him that I had chosen correctly. He doubted I would stick with it and it turned out he was right. When I told him I was resigning so I could raise the girls myself, he simply sighed and said, 'Of course you are.'"

She snorted at the memory. "At least he finally began to understand why as he watched them grow. He was always traveling when I was a child so I think by watching me with the girls he realized how much he missed." She paused and shook her head. "Yet here I am again, poised to disappoint him once more by wanting to quit staying home and go back to work. I guess he was right all along. I can't stick to anything."

Shock careened over Anne's face. That was the absolute last thing she ever expected to hear come out of Lindsay's mouth. "You not being able to stick to anything? That's a crock!" she exclaimed. "You are happily married and have been for eleven years. You graduated college and law school. You worked your butt off and won the most prestigious scholarship, so law school was even completely paid for.

"So what if you decide you need a change in careers? People do that all the time and are never accused of being wishy-washy. Your plans and interests change. That does not make you any less of a devoted mother and wife, or less of a professional."

She paused in her speech to lift Lindsay's chin with a caring finger. Her voice softened as Lindsay's disbelieving eyes met her own. "In fact, I admire your choices. You left your career at its height, placing a greater priority on your family. Now that the girls are in school, you have the flexibility to return to it. Who wouldn't think of that as having your cake and eating it, too? The furthest thing from the truth is that you can't stick to anything!

"And as for disappointing your father, those were his dreams, not yours. That disappointment is his, not yours. You are called to walk the road you are called to walk. So your earthly father's dreams didn't match your heavenly Father's plans? Guess whose needed a realignment?" she asked with a compassionate smile.

Lindsay sat motionless, her stunned gaze telling Anne better than words that her lecture and unwavering support had just slayed a powerful dragon in her life. Anne tugged Lindsay closer as cleansing tears filled her eyes and washed away the lies she had unwittingly nurtured for almost two decades. Joy surged through her as the fears Lindsay had given safe harbor were unmoored. Her best friend was free.

Chapter 14

Later that evening, Anne sat on her bed, pondering the souvenirs she had purchased for each of her children. Something was wrong, but she had no idea what it could be. She had easily and happily chosen a pirate costume for Theo, complete with rapier sword, knowing he would swashbuckle his way through the backyard and love every minute.

For Kelsie, though, she had made a serious and sober consideration of several items. After much contemplation, Anne had opted for a puzzle of local marine life, with the animal names printed in English and Latin, knowing that was an upcoming topic for her daughter's grade. Kelsie was already having difficulty with the sciences, and Anne knew she would need the support to achieve her fondest wish: for Kelsie to become a doctor or a researcher.

With a start, Anne blinked. *Her* wish for Kelsie. Where had she heard that before? An icy douse of reality crashed through her. Only a few hours ago, Anne had comforted and cradled the victim of another well-intentioned parent's dreams, supporting her friend's choices and aspirations in the face of her father's hopes and plans. That memory now accused Anne of the same crime with blatant accuracy. After all, wasn't she doing exactly what Robert Duncan had done—pushing her daughter into something she might or might not be interested in doing—just because that was what she wanted for Kelsie? *Wow. Talk about pot and kettle.*

That knowledge in hand, Anne was forced to ponder questions she had never thought to ask. When had she started pushing Kelsie to follow her path rather than find the one God had specifically in mind for the girl? When had she decided that Kelsie should be interested in the sciences instead of watching and listening to discover the girl's talents and dreams and supporting those? For that matter, did she even know what Kelsie was interested in outside of pop music? When was the last time she had simply sat down and listened, even if it was to the silence between them? Anne thought back over the last few months and couldn't name a single interaction that she hadn't initiated, continued, and ended. No wonder Kelsie rarely spoke to her. There was no room for her daughter to get a word in edgewise with Anne's running commentary, which she fully admitted was often more critical than necessary.

Her own mother had behaved in a similar manner when Anne was Kelsie's age, pushing music and math classes. Doris Jackson had hoped to develop her daughter's logic skills with an eye toward an academic or medical career. It didn't seem to matter that Anne hadn't wanted to play the flute and wasn't interested in calculus and trigonometry. Anne had complied, but now began to wonder if, without her mother's constant pressure, she would have stayed in the band all through high school? Would she have taken all of the upper-level math courses?

Anne's brow furrowed as she picked up Theo's pirate costume. So, if she pushed Kelsie, why didn't Theo feel the same pressure? Anne thought back to those early years of her childhood and never once in any of those memories did she recall her mother badgering David, Anne's younger brother. Perhaps David had put a stop to it early on, and Anne had never had the courage to thwart her mother's plans like Lindsay had done with her father.

A stray memory popped into her head. At the beginning of sophomore year of high school, she had been demoted to second chair from first chair by an incoming freshman, and her mother had gone ballistic on her and the band director right after school. Mortified and shamed by her mother's words, Anne had angrily asked why she was so hard on her and not on David. He hadn't made the middle school football team, and her mother had said nothing about it.

The answer had silenced any further arguments or questions. Doris Jackson had always wanted to be a doctor but had to settle for nursing school because, in the Deep South, it wasn't considered appropriate for a woman to go to medical school. Women were wives, secretaries, teachers, and nurses. Her mother had said that David would have more and better opportunities afforded to him just because he was male, while

Anne was handicapped by her sex. So she said she pushed Anne in order for her to be the best option for whatever job she wanted, in spite of the fact she was female.

Anne shook her head and sighed. Like Lindsay's father, her mother was well-intentioned, but that didn't make it right. It also didn't excuse Anne's own behavior, learned or not. The last thing she wanted was for Kelsie to continue the cycle with her own daughter when the time came. The time to end it was now, but how?

She tapped the puzzle, considering her own actions and her daughter's desires. One had to give in order for the other to thrive. A verse from a recent sermon on Second Chronicles whispered through her, something about humbling oneself and God healing their land.

She pulled her phone from where it lay on the other side of the bed and opened her Bible app. A quick keyword search directed her to Second Chronicles 7:14: "If my people who are called by My name humble themselves, pray and seek My face, and turn from their evil ways, then I will hear from heaven, forgive their sin, and heal their land."

Anne closed her eyes, allowing the words to flow over and into her, putting into practice the reflection skills she had learned the day before. Perhaps this was the answer to her prayers: the need to humble herself and her ideas in favor of God's plans for Kelsie.

"Anne!" Jess called from downstairs. "Are you ready to go to dinner?"

Anne tapped the phone's screen to bookmark the verse and, with an understanding smile, looked once more at Kelsie's souvenir. Certainty flooded her, and she called back to Jess, "Yes, but I need to make a stop first!" Grabbing the puzzle and her purse, which held the receipt, she hurried out, filled with the heady mixture of relief and dawning awareness.

Delia reached the Coleman Pavilion in Seaside a few minutes before five and found Max waiting for her once more. She chuckled and shook her head. He was obviously an early bird. His gaze caught hers, and she tried to hide the amused smile, but he grinned at her and, wanting to share in her humor, asked, “What’s so funny?”

She shook her head again. “Nothing really. You’re early again. Is that a habit, or are you just that eager to see me?” Delia inwardly blanched at the forthright question. Never in her life had she been that bold.

Max grabbed her hand and tugged her down beside him on the bench, then rested his arm behind her. He turned and slipped a slow, pleased smile across his lips. “Both?” he suggested as a teasing light danced in his green eyes. The breeze picked up a lock of her hair and swooped it across her face, but Max easily tucked it back behind her ear with his free hand.

Delia shivered as his fingers grazed her cheek. *What is it about this man?* She wasn’t nervous, but her heart pounded and her breath caught with that simple touch. Instinctively, she stayed his hand with her own and snuggled her cheek into his palm, closing her eyes to savor the feel of his roughened skin. Delia heard his breath catch in surprise and opened her eyes.

An unfamiliar light darkened his gaze, startling her with the complexity of greens and golds that flickered in its depths. Unthinking, she moistened her suddenly too-dry lips and watched his gaze drop to them. She realized in that moment that they were quickly treading into deeper waters than she had planned, and she pulled his hand from her cheek. Rising abruptly, she tugged him up behind her and tossed a too-jaunty, “Let’s go see the beach,” over her shoulder.

She felt him follow along, her hand still tucked in his, as their feet sank down into the deep, sugar-white sand of the beach access. A few steps later, Delia paused to pull off her flip-flops and watched him do the same out of the corner of her eye. The light breeze soothed her reddened cheeks as the wave-packed sand cooled her soles. She shot Max a surreptitious glance and, seeing he had recovered from her inadvertent advance, Delia cleared her throat and prompted, “So, um, you said you were from South Carolina?”

Max nodded and squeezed her hand, silently thanking her for the opening. “Estill, a blink-and-you-miss-it town of about two thousand people,” he said as he tugged his Costa sunglasses from around the back of his neck. Though it was early evening, the glare of the sun against the sand remained formidable. Delia took the hint and pulled her own from the top of her head and settled them into place. "As a kid, I couldn't wait to get away and be me rather than the son of Harrison Andrews and the future company boss. I needed my own identity. Does that make sense?" he asked, vulnerability pursing his lips in a half-smile, half-frown.

Delia nodded, completely able to empathize with needing to escape from small-town life. She squeezed his hand in support, urging him to continue. She didn't have to wait long. "When I look back on it now, that map dot was the best place to grow up." He paused as if memories rather than waves and seagulls suddenly filled his vision. "I was surrounded by family and a community that loved God and me. And it was that family and that community that welcomed me home with open arms when my dad died."

Max shook his head and swallowed hard. Delia felt a wave of sympathy crash over her. He obviously had loved his father very much. After a moment, his tear-roughed voice continued, "His death made me take a hard look at the life I had created for myself, and I didn't like a lot of what I found. Oh, sure, I was tremendously successful by the world's standards: a six-figure paycheck, a high-priced sports car, a fancy condo. But inside I was spiritually bankrupt."

They walked in silence for a moment steadily approaching a young family. Max studied the two toddlers, who squatted by a haphazard sandcastle, their mother watching from under a colorful beach umbrella. The breaking waves and cawing seagulls accented their playful cries. He cleared his throat and said, "When I went to USC for college, I ran absolutely wild. It was the most freedom I had ever had up until that point in my life. No one knew who I was. I had no family tradition or heritage to live up to, and I took full advantage of the anonymity. When my college girlfriend failed her pregnancy test, I did the honorable thing, and against everyone's wishes back home, I married her. My parents wanted her to give the baby up for adoption rather than us marry at such a young age, but I wouldn't hear of it. It was my responsibility and a rude awakening to adulthood."

He paused, absorbing his own evaluation of the time and, Delia thought, preparing himself for the words that followed. "She lost the baby a couple of months later, and we tried to make it last. I was graduating, and she had a year left. We were so young, and our lives were going in such different directions that we divorced after eleven months." Guilt rested heavily on him, slumping his shoulders with its weight.

Max took in a fortifying breath and plowed on with the story. "So there I was, just graduated college, a failed marriage, no child, and so filled with shame that I couldn't face the family that I believed I had disappointed by my choices. I did the only thing I knew to do since my guilt and pride wouldn't let me return home. I got a great sales position with an international company based in D.C., and I threw myself into it. For ten years, I traveled the globe and made lots of money, but then one day I got a call from Mom. Dad had died suddenly. Heart attack at his desk. As awful as this sounds, it was actually the best thing that could have happened to me. Sure, we had talked on the phone and e-mailed over the years, but it took returning home for the funeral for me to realize how far I had drifted away from my faith and my roots.

"So, I quit my job in D.C. and moved back, finally ready and able to appreciate my heritage. I took over the company just as my father had always wanted." He sighed and let the monologue lapse as his thoughts once more turned inward to process all he had said.

After a moment, Delia prompted, "So you were back in the fold? The prodigal had returned, and everything was good?"

Max considered her words, then nodded. "There was some adjustment, but yeah, everything was mostly smooth professionally. My faith, though, was another story. I was very angry at my dad's death. When I got back, I again threw myself into work rather than deal with the emotional fallout. I wanted nothing to do with the faith of my family. But all that angry rebellion and self-righteousness did was allow me to find out about God for myself.

"I remember sitting at what had been my dad's desk one night and going through the financials. I caught a glance of a picture of him, my mom, and me that he had on a bookshelf from when I was in high school. We were so happy and, I don't know, I just lost it. Me sitting at his desk without him looking over my shoulder and teaching me the ropes—that wasn't how it was supposed to be. I shoved all the papers off the desk at the unfairness of it all and cried like a baby. I was so glad I was the last one at the office." His wry chuckle was caught by the breeze and drifted away seconds after she heard it. But it was enough time for her to squeeze his hand in silent support.

"That night I yelled and screamed at God, venting out all of the emotions that I had held in—even back to college and the divorce. How could the God I knew in childhood allow all of that to happen? I had to have cried for at least an hour. When it was over, I realized that all I knew about God was what my parents and the church had told me as I was growing up. I really didn't know Him for myself. He was like the kindly uncle only seen at family reunions. Everyone told me about Him, how wonderful and caring He was, but I didn't know any of that personally. So I took a hard look at who I had been told He was versus who He really was to me. I've got to say, it shattered a lot of misconceptions. Now I can honestly say that I have my own faith, not the faith of my parents."

They walked on in silence once more, each enjoying the company and the revelations. A verse from Romans popped into Delia's head, and she murmured, "All things work together for good for those who love God and are called according to His purpose."

A rumbling *hmm* tickled the air between them as Max considered her words.

Delia added, "I told you we were here for a women's retreat, right?" He nodded, and she continued, "The first part of it was reflection. It's what the teacher called a faith builder. You pick a verse and think about how it has happened in your life. And your situation with your father's death fits that verse to a tee."

"Yeah, I guess you're right," Max replied. "Dad's death brought me back to the faith and to the family business, which was always in my heart to run." He paused as if looking at the whole scene through a different lens. "I think he would have liked that."

He slowed their amble then turned them back toward Seaside. With a wry chuckle, he said, "Well now, here I've done what all good Southerners and salesman do and talked the entire time. Tell me about you."

"Oh," Delia answered with a slight blush stealing across her cheeks.

"Well, I'm from a similar map dot but not such a happy childhood. There was no faith in my house, and I never thought to question why." She paused and decided to steer clear of the bullying and abuse, saving that conversation for another time and place. She stopped suddenly in her tracks and looked up at him, wonder in her gaze and peace in her soul. There would be another opportunity to tell Max. She would be seeing him again in spite of her impending departure for Fairhope.

Max turned as her hand slipped from his own and, bemused by her silent appraisal, asked, "Delia?"

An all-encompassing grin split her features, and she shook her head.

Max held out his hand to her, and as hers met its strength and surety, a sense of homecoming washed through her. Tears pricked the corners of her eyes, and she shook her head again. She squeezed his hand and said, "Everything's perfect."

Relief flooded his gaze. With an easy grace, he lifted their joined hands to his lips and kissed her knuckles. "I'm so glad," he replied as he tugged her back to walking.

Chapter 15

Anne stepped down the stairs from Seaside's combined book and record store and spied Lindsay and Jess seated at a picnic table on the patio of Southern Kitchen. The pale green umbrella shading the table from the lowering sun perfectly accented the building's white clapboard and tin roof. A side porch housing the bar faced her. Lindsay leaned over the deck railing as Anne approached and said, "Hey, the entrance is over there. We just ordered drinks. I put in a water for you since I didn't think you'd want anything more than that."

"No, that's perfect for this late in the day," Anne confirmed. "Any more caffeine and I won't sleep tonight." She soon joined them at the table and smiled at the waitress as she delivered the drinks.

"Welcome to Southern Kitchen," she said. "I'll give y'all a few minutes to look over the menu and be back shortly."

"That would be great," Jess replied, then asked Anne, "So, did you find something good?"

Anne nodded. "I found a poster I'm fairly sure she'll like. You know, it's funny. When I first read the flyer for the retreat, I felt something in me tell me I had to come, but I never would have expected this result."

"I was praying I would find an answer even if it wasn't the one I wanted to hear," Jess said. "Getting away helped me to shut out the distractions and focus on hearing what God was telling me all along."

"I can definitely agree about the getting away," Lindsay said. "Y'all had to practically drag me here, but it was exactly what I needed to get insight and perspective."

Anne smiled. "And then there's Deli! Talk about unexpected!"

"I wonder what he's like," Lindsay mused. "She's been in the clouds since they met."

Jess took a sip of her tea and shrugged. "All I know is he called her Delia, and she was absolutely bowled over."

"He called her that?" Anne asked, her eyebrows disappearing into her hairline. As surprising as that detail was, the reason was even more perplexing. "That means she introduced herself as Delia."

Jess nodded. "Yeah, I was shocked, too. But I guess that reflection verse really spoke to her."

"So, should we start calling her Delia?" Lindsay asked as she took a sip of her own tea.

"I asked her about that, and she said she'd like it," Jess replied with a sweet, proud smile.

"Wow," Lindsay breathed. "Talk about a growth spurt!"

Anne raised her water glass toward the middle of the table and toasted, "To Delia!"

"To Delia!" Jess and Lindsay chimed with a chuckle.

As they each took a sip to celebrate, the waitress returned, ready to take their orders. After a few minutes of discussion of preferences and specialties, they each settled on a different dish so they could sample more of the menu.

"So, how are the girls liking their weekend with their grandparents?" Anne asked Lindsay as the other woman pulled silverware and napkins from the white bucket at the end of the table.

Lindsay handed a set to Jess then Anne and replied, "Loving it! I wouldn't be surprised if this becomes a regular request from both parties. John said he got so much done Friday that he was able to take a break today and get in a round of golf with some of his buddies from church. All that's left are some finishing touches on the presentation, and he's waiting to hear back from a coworker for them; then he'll be ready to go."

"That's great news, Lindsay!" Jess said as she reached for her tea glass.

"So, Jess," Anne began, "any word from Mitch today?"

Jess shook her head as she took a sip. "No, but I didn't really expect to hear from him, what with the game and tailgating and all. When he's watching it at my house, I can barely get two words out of him that aren't football related." She paused and twirled her straw, stirring the ice cubes in her rapidly disappearing tea. "His whole devotion to football is actually one of the things that I took a hard look at this weekend."

Lindsay furrowed her brow. "How so?"

"Y'all know he goes to church with me, but he doesn't go because he wants to. Even though he was raised in the church, he doesn't place God as a priority in his life. Everything else, especially Alabama football, comes before God, and every time I mention men's Bible studies or him taking a more active role in building his faith, he always has something else to do. Something that's more important." She sighed. "You know I hate to say this, but I'm not even sure he's saved."

Anne reached over and laid a hand on Jess's forearm. "I'm sure God is working in him in His own way."

Jess nodded sadly. "I'm sure He is, but Mitch is beginning to hint around that he wants to get married. Anne, you and Ted, and Lindsay, you and John, have provided me with such wonderful models of what a godly marriage is supposed to be that, knowing what I know of Mitch's priorities, I've come to realize that I just can't accept when he does propose."

Lindsay grimaced in sympathy. "One thing you have to keep in mind, Jess, is that even the best marriages have hard times, but you are absolutely right about needing a compatible level of faith. That should be the basis for a marriage in order to get through the worse in the 'for better or worse.'"

"Marriage is a partnership, and it is work," Anne commented. "But I wouldn't trade my life for anything. Ted and I just knew even in high school that we were it. Our faiths grew as we experienced the highs and lows together."

Their waitress arrived with a tray of plates in one hand and a folding table in the other. "Here we are, ladies!" she said as she began setting entrées down in front of each of them. "Everything look good?"

The ladies each glanced at their plates and smiled appreciatively. "Looks great," Anne said.

"Great! I'll be back to check on you in a bit. Oh, and I'll bring around some more tea and water."

Lindsay nodded her thanks, then turned to the others. "Time to play Split the Plate!" she said as she began to divide up her shrimp and grits into three servings. The others followed suit, and soon their murmurs of pleasure filled the table.

After a few bites, Anne said, “Getting back to the topic at hand, Jess. Ted and I grew together, but based on what you’re saying, that’s not really an option that you see available for you and Mitch, right?”

Jess nodded as she chewed on a bite of shrimp macaroni and cheese. “This weekend helped me realize that I’m not called to walk him through growing his faith. I need to let Mitch go. Who knows? Maybe the breakup is what he needs to jog him out of his complacency and encourage him to find God for himself. At least that’s what I’m praying will happen. The last thing I want is for Mitch to walk away from faith completely because I’m choosing God over him. I really need y’all to pray that I’ll have the right words when we get back.”

Lindsay grabbed Jess’s hand as well as Anne’s. “There’s no time like the present!” she said with an encouraging smile. “Lord, we come before You to ask for Your wisdom for Jess. You know her heart is not to hurt Mitch, but she also knows that this is Your will. Give her the words she needs when the time comes. And above all, we put Mitch and her in the palm of Your hand, where we know You will care for them and cover them. Thank you, Lord. In Jesus’s name. Amen.”

“Amen,” Jess and Anne chorused.

Jess squeezed the others’ hands and then released them. “Thank you, both, so very much.

~~*

On the opposite side of Central Square and across 30A, Max and Delia were seated at a rooftop table overlooking the Gulf. Max had recommended the snapper and the scallops, which made the choice easy for Delia. Now munching on her scallops and grits, she silently mused at the perfection of the day. Max took a bite of his fish then prompted, “So, you said you’re a travel writer. Did you always want to be a journalist?”

Delia smiled and shrugged. “I guess. I fell in love with my english and journalism classes in high school. They were a way to disappear, you know?” She answered with a wry twist of her lips. Max’s gaze sharpened at her words, his intrigue evident. Delia opted not to spoil the joy of the moment with the darkness of the past, so she sidestepped his unspoken question. "The more I studied, the more I longed to go to Northwestern—they have an award-winning journalism department—and then work for the *Chicago Tribune*. I was able to get a full ride, compliments of the university, and various scholarships, which allowed me to go. There was no way my parents could have afforded it otherwise. Once I got to college, I was like a pig in slop."

She blushed furiously as she realized her description wasn't the most socially acceptable. "I mean I was absolutely at home," she finished lamely to the tune of Max's delighted chuckle.

"No doubt about it, you're a Southern girl, Delia Preston."

"Arkansas Razorback born and bred," she said. "I guess you can take the girl out of the country, but—"

"You can't take the country out of the girl," they chorused.

Max laughed good-naturedly and raised his glass to her. "And here's to not wanting to!"

Delia shook her head and clinked her glass to his. "Oh, I don't know about that. There were so many times when I longed to be rid of my childhood map dot and all that went with it—including the dialect and jargon. But over time and as I began to travel around the country and even outside of it, I began to appreciate my Southern raising a bit more."

"How did you get into travel writing?" he asked as he put his glass down after taking a healthy swig of the tea. "Was it a big adjustment from the *Trib*?"

"Not really," she answered as she sliced into a succulent scallop. "I started at the *Trib* as a field reporter, covering everything and anything, and finally worked my way up to the occasional Op-Ed piece, but I guess part of me romanticized the whole life of a journalist. That dream just got deflated one story after another as I was assigned topics that either didn't interest me or ran contrary to my faith.

"I had become a Christian in college. My roommate actually led me to Christ, and when I graduated and got a job, I was buffeted by such varying morals and inconsistent beliefs and ideologies, I knew it wasn't an environment that I wanted to be in forever. About five years after I started at the *Trib*, I received an e-mail. At first I brushed it off because it looked like one of those spam-type headhunting kinds." He nodded as he took a bite of his snapper. "Well, it said there was a travel writer position open with a publishing group based out of Atlanta. A new magazine was being started up, and the editor was searching for writers. When I asked a bit more, I was told I could pick or decline topics of my choosing, and all travel was paid for either by the publisher or by the site I was visiting, especially if it was a requested write-up, so I jumped at it. Gave my two-week notice and immediately started to look for an apartment in Atlanta."

"So how did you end up in Fairhope from Atlanta?"

"It was love," Delia admitted with a smile. At Max's slightly stricken look, she laughed and said, "No, not that kind of love. I was there to profile their annual arts and crafts festival for a write-up and fell in love with the city. Between Chicago and Atlanta, I'd had my fill of big cities—all the noise, all the people, all the traffic!" She shuddered. "I don't know, I just drove into Fairhope, and it felt like home. So I talked it over with my employer, and they said since my job didn't require me to be in Atlanta except for meetings, I was free to relocate wherever I saw fit.

"I bought my first house, and now I travel anywhere from two to three weeks out the month." She paused to take a sip of her tea, then mused, "It's funny. No matter where or how often I travel, I always feel comforted when I see that 'Welcome to Fairhope' sign. I'll have been there four years this coming April."

The waiter appeared beside the table to ask about dessert preferences, which neither desired, and Max asked for the check. Tab paid a few minutes later, he escorted her down the exterior stairs and into the open market that paralleled the beach. The sun ended its dip into the horizon, and suddenly the lights in the trees along Airstream Row blinked on, lighting the path for pedestrians and bicyclists alike.

Delia paused at the crosswalk and turned to Max. The teasing light in his eyes was accompanied by a sincere question. "Mind if I walk you home?" he asked.

Delia returned his smile and shook her head. "I thought you'd never ask." She grabbed his hand and tugged him across the street.

They walked around Central Square in silence, absorbing the calls of the kids as they tumbled and chased each other in the amphitheater green. After a few minutes, Max cleared his throat. Delia glanced up at him, curious, and seeing his serious look, knew something was on his mind. She had an idea though, given that tomorrow she would be heading home, and their weekend would be over.

"You know, when I first saw you on the bridge, I thought, *My God, that's a beautiful woman.* But then, when we started talking, it was more than that. There was something about you that I couldn't explain. I just knew I needed to see you again, and I prayed that you would come back that afternoon. Matter of fact, that's the hardest I've prayed since that night in my dad's office. And this afternoon, I know I probably shared so much more than I should have for a second date, but I just couldn't shake the feeling that I had to lay everything out—all the cards on the table, as it were."

They passed the bike rack where she and the others had parked their bikes Thursday evening when they had first begun to explore Seaside, and Delia marveled at how much had changed in the space of forty-eight hours. "I was glad you did, Max. I was actually amazed that somehow you knew everything that I wanted to ask you." She chuckled lightly. "I have to say, you're the easiest interview I've ever done."

He smiled and winked at her then drew her hand to his lips.

All too soon, she paused their stroll at the foot of the steps to Betty's cottage. "This is me," Delia admitted reluctantly, not yet ready to end the night.

Max glanced at the door and then licked his lips as if weighing his next words. "You know. I did this whole thing so wrong with Katie, my ex, and I swore to myself if you came back yesterday to paddle I would do everything in my power to do it right with you, not move too fast or go too far. But—" he paused, obviously waging an internal battle with propriety and timing "—I really want to kiss you right now." His voice dropped to a whisper as he implored, "Please say that's okay."

Eyes locked onto his, Delia slowly nodded.

Max trailed his fingers along her hairline, brushing her ebony curls back, and she closed her eyes as the simple pleasure of his touch skittered through her nerve endings. She felt his breath a heartbeat before his lips, and then she was soaring as sensation poured into her—sweet, heady, and unlike anything she had ever experienced.

He lifted his mouth from hers a moment later, lips clinging, loathe to end their joining. Max cleared his throat and rested his forehead against hers. "Wow," he breathed. "Now I know what Louis Armstrong meant."

"What?" Delia whispered, unwilling to break the moment.

A beautiful smile lit his eyes as he framed her face with both hands. "A kiss to build a dream on."

She opened her mouth to respond just as the porch light clicked on. Startled, they both jumped a bit, and Delia, thinking the others stood on the other side of the window, noses pressed to the glass, glanced back to the door with a shy smile. While there were no noses, a set of fingers did wiggle in her direction in a friendly, if knowing, wave. She shook her head, feeling a bit like a teenager, home from a first date. The heat of embarrassment rose up from her neck, sending her face into the crook of his shoulder.

The position did have its benefits. The air around her, once filled with the aroma of pine, was saturated with the sandalwood and musk of Max's cologne. Delia slowly inhaled, basking in the comforting maleness of the scent. She turned her head, laying her cheek against his shoulder, and his arms wrapped loosely around her. "Come to church with us tomorrow?" The words were out of her mouth before she could stop them.

Before she could flinch or backpedal, Max replied softly, "Love to." He dropped a kiss to the bridge of her nose then tucked his cheek against her forehead. They stood snuggled together until another unexpected interruption once again broke them apart: Max's cell phone. It buzzed in his back pocket. Incessantly.

With a groan and a gentle squeeze before releasing her, he tugged the phone out and grimaced. "I'm sorry, but I've got to call him back now. It's a buyer."

Delia smiled and shook her head. "Don't worry about it. I probably need to go in before they start sneaking around from the back to check on us."

Max flashed that sweet, boyish grin, and Delia's heart flipped over. "This does remind me, though," he said, lifting the phone, "that I need to give you my number." He paused and raised a hand to her cheek. Brushing his thumb against her cheekbone, he added, "I don't want to lose contact with you, Delia."

Delia shifted a bit to kiss his palm and answered, "Me neither." Pulling her own phone out of her back pocket, she gave him her number and added, "I never switched when I moved from Atlanta."

Max tapped the number into his phone, then tapped a bit more before hitting send. "I'll be here tomorrow at nine forty-five. We can all walk over together."

"Sounds perfect. See you in the morning," she whispered. Her phone buzzed with his incoming text message, and Max slipped away as she looked down to retrieve it.

Delia blushed rosily and swore she could hear his drawl in her head.

Chapter 16

The Road Home

Jess slid her suitcase closer to the edge of the bed and plopped a stack of clothes into one side of it, saving room for her makeup case and the extra pairs of sandals she had brought. She pursed her lips as she pondered where her new Seaside sweatshirt would fit and finally decided to just keep it in the shopping bag. Even though Lindsay had purchased several things for her family, there would still be plenty of room in her trunk.

Jess's phone dinged with an incoming message. She glanced toward where it lay on the nightstand and saw it was merely a news notification. A relieved sigh passed between her lips, knowing there was a text that remained unanswered, hidden in the apps.

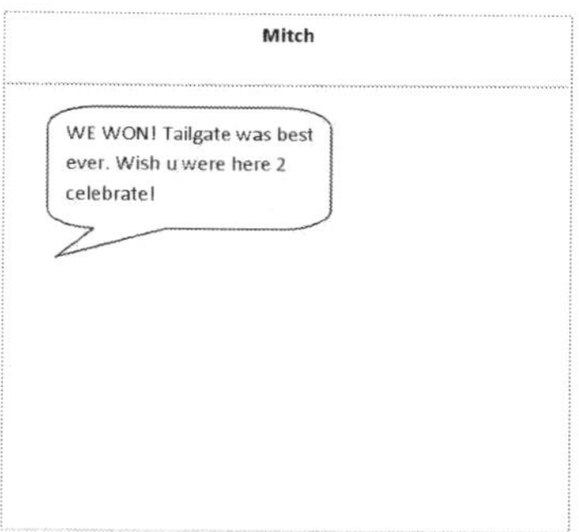

When it had come through the night before, she had read the preview as it popped up on the screen, but she hadn't gotten any further, knowing her phone was set to send read receipts. Even though she had expected to hear from Mitch and was at peace with her decision, Jess just wasn't ready to respond yet. A light tap on her door barely registered as she continued to contemplate the phone and its contents.

"Jess?" Delia prompted. "Jess, you in here?" The second question was louder, so Jess knew Delia had poked her head around the door.

She shook the dreary thoughts from her head and answered, "Yeah, just getting everything packed."

"Hey," Delia replied, concern softening her tone. "You okay?"

Jess shrugged and nodded then picked up one of the sandals and toyed with the strap. "Yeah, I guess." With a heavy sigh, she plopped onto the bed. "Delia, this is the pits."

Delia leaned against the doorjamb and frowned. "Mitch, right? And I'm guessing by your mood that you're going to end it when you get back?"

"I have to," Jess admitted with a helpless wave of her hand. "It's not fair to either of us to continue when I know the result will be the same regardless of how long I wait. The thing of it is, I do care for him a great deal, and the last thing I want is to hurt him. But I know that's all this is going to do."

"You know, sweetie," Delia began as she pushed off the doorjamb and joined Jess on the bed. "I read somewhere that there's a big difference between hurting and harming someone. Things, especially something like this, will cause pain or hurt, but it won't damage him beyond repair. Growth is often painful, but it doesn't kill us." She paused and linked their hands together. "Besides, how he reacts is his choice; you're not responsible for that. The only thing that is your responsibility is to tell him the truth in love. God can handle the rest."

Jess nudged Delia's shoulder in thanks. "Keep telling me that. I'm sure I'll need the reminder the closer we get to home." Shaking off the doldrums, she flashed a teasing smile at her friend. "So, we get to meet the mystery man today, hmm? Can you at least tell us his name before he gets here, so we don't make fools of ourselves?"

Delia had the good grace to blush at the teasing rebuke. "It's Max Andrews. He's from Estill, South Carolina, and he runs his family's saw mill company. Anything else you want to know?"

"Hmm," Jess pondered, an impish light gleaming in her eyes. "Do you melt when he kisses you?"

"Jess!" Delia cried as her whole upper body pinked a clear shade of rose.

Jess giggled at Delia's embarrassment. "Okay, too personal, I admit." She paused and grew serious. "Does he make you feel as special as you are?"

Delia couldn't hide the grin of delight that radiated from her face. "More."

"That's all I needed to know," Jess answered with a fond smile.

The doorbell rang, and a duet of delighted squeals echoed from downstairs, where Anne and Lindsay were finishing their coffee and tea. "Deeelllyaah," Lindsay sang up the stairs, "he's heeerrre!"

Delia turned, and Jess knew her face matched their friends' voices. She chuckled at the thought and shook her head in amazement at how quickly fully grown women could disintegrate into teenagers when a man came into the picture.

Delia eyeballed Jess and warned with mock severity, "Don't you start, too!"

Jess shrugged and, with a wide-eyed look of innocence, proclaimed, "Did I say anything?" Her virtuosity was quickly belied by a snicker that bubbled up and followed Delia as she left the room.

~~*

Delia opened the front door and almost swallowed her tongue. The man who stood in front of her was definitely Max, but most certainly not the stubble-cheeked, shorts and Vineyard Vines T-shirt version. This man sported a pale sage-green linen shirt with khaki dress shorts and a clean-shaven face, looking for all the world as if he had just stepped out of a men's fashion magazine. "H-h-hi!" she managed to spurt out. She could feel the twin gazes of Anne and Lindsay peering around her to scope out the new addition to the front stoop. "Um, yeah, come in," she finally said as she grabbed his hand and tugged him across the threshold.

However, she forgot to tell her feet that they needed to move as well, and Max was forced to engulf her in a hug to keep both of them from falling on the floor. He chuckled as he kissed her cheek. "Morning, darlin'," he drawled softly into her ear. She shuddered at the comforting warmth of his arms and the accompanying intimacy of his greeting.

It was a good thing they had company because she couldn't be held responsible for her response otherwise.

"Morning, handsome," she greeted, somehow finding the words in her stunned mind, then blushed at her too-honest evaluation of his appearance.

"So, you must be Max," Delia heard Jess say from somewhere over by the stairs.

Grateful for the rescue, she turned and threw a thankful look to Jess then said, "Yes, girls, this is Max. Max this is Lindsay, Anne, and Jess. My friends."

Max nodded to each in turn and then replied, "It's a pleasure to meet y'all. But I must say, I haven't heard much about any of y'all."

"The same could be said for you," Lindsay said. "Delia has been on cloud nine since y'all met." A sudden sharp jab of Anne's elbow into her side had Lindsay whispering, "What? She has been!"

Jess shook her head and rolled her eyes at the other two. "Ignore them," she said with good-natured humor. "They're pleased to meet you as well." She tossed a speaking glance their way and nodded toward where their purses lay on the couch. "We should probably be going if we want to get seats inside."

"Yes, definitely!" Anne chimed in. "But Jane said they moved the benches from the park for added seating outdoors."

"So, do we walk or take the bikes?" Lindsay asked the group as she tucked her purse under her arm and handed Anne her own.

"Well, I would say that all depends on where y'all would like to eat lunch after church," Max offered. "My treat. There are a few restaurants within walking distance, but there's a neat little wine bar in WaterColor that has a nice brunch menu. It is a bit of a hike, though, so taking the bikes would be the best."

Delia glanced at the others and, seeing their agreement, replied, "That sounds lovely. Bikes it is!"

~~*

By the time the church bell tolled, the chapel was comfortably full inside. The ladies had opted for seats toward the middle. Max was seated on the end, next to Delia. The group was warmly welcomed by the locals who regularly attended, a few of whom Anne and Lindsay recognized from the retreat. The regular worship pastor was back at the music stand, and a lovely montage of hymns rang out from his harmonica as the congregation was called to worship.

A few minutes and a chorus of contemporary worship songs later, Greg, Jane's husband and the chapel's pastor, stood up and warmly greeted the congregation. "Welcome to the Courtyard Chapel. Before you get seated, turn to your neighbor and tell them, 'Happy Sunday!'" Each person complied, and a few minutes of loud voices reigned prior to everyone settling back in the pews.

"This weekend, the Courtyard Chapel hosted our first ladies' retreat. Can I get a show of hands of the ladies who are here today that attended?" Several women answered his request, and a few added a smattering of applause. "That is great! My wife, Jane, told me it was a huge success, and we are hoping this will be an annual event, so y'all will all have to come back next year and bring your friends!

"We're actually going to build a bit on the topics of reflecting and meditating on God's Word, which was the subject of the retreat, but we're going to look more generally at why we are called to study and know God's Word. The psalmist says, 'Your word I have hidden in my heart,' and why did he do that? He says, 'So I won't sin against you.' In order to keep our relationship with God free from as many pitfalls and stumbling blocks as we possibly can, it is important to read, study, and learn His Word."

Greg began to unpack the topic, incorporating comments and answers from the congregation as he usually did in his sermons, and within an hour, he was dismissing the group with Matt, the worship leader, adding the blessing, "Travel mercies," for those who would be returning home.

~~*

Max led the group as they threaded their way out the front door and stopped to greet the pastor and Jane, thanking them for the lovely service and for hosting the retreat. Unable to say much more, given the other attendees who waited behind them, the quintet unlocked their bikes. He gave general directions to the wine bar then confidently pedaled off, Delia happily riding beside him.

They rode along the back side of Central Square, dodging other cyclists and pedestrians alike until Max paused in front of a house on Natchez Street. Delia sent him a questioning look, and he winked in response, his conspiratorial grin warming her more effectively than the Florida sun. "Y'all ever see the movie *The Truman Show*?" he asked as he turned on his seat to see the others' reactions.

Delia nodded, awareness suddenly dawning, but not wanting to ruin the surprise for the others. He had mentioned it in passing as they had walked back through Seaside to the restaurant the night before

"It's been a while, but, yeah," Jess replied for the group.

"Well," Max replied with a nod, "this was his house in the movie."

Lindsay looked a bit perplexed. "What do you mean? Is it based on the house in the movie?"

"Nope, the whole movie was filmed right here in Seaside. As a matter of fact, the community's school was built from the money the production company paid in order to use the town."

Anne shook her head in wonder. "That's amazing. I'm going to have to rewatch that movie and see how many places I recognize. I'm surprised Betty never mentioned it. I wonder if she was here during the filming?"

"You'll have to ask when we get back," Lindsay said as she set her feet to her bike pedals. "Let's go! I'm getting hungry, and I can't wait to interrogate Max!"

A few minutes later, as they reached the boundary between Seaside and WaterColor, Max paused the group again. Curious as to whether the others needed to catch up, Delia glanced back and only then realized why he had stopped. The difference between the two communities was more palpable than most state borders. Certainly there was the tricolored sign proclaiming the impending entrance into WaterColor, but the change of scenery as pine straw and grass replaced gravel for ground covering was a clear line of demarcation. Up ahead, the houses were much more muted than the candied pastels of Seaside and almost blended into their surrounds, enhancing the idea of nature and development coexisting in a cordial balance. The words *effortless*, *organic*, and *serene* slipped into Delia's travel writer brain as she absorbed the disparity.

"Wow," Jess remarked. "Talk about a big difference."

Max nodded. "There are actually eleven beach towns along 30A, each with its own distinctive atmosphere. Grayton Beach and Seagrove are the oldest, and Seaside was the first planned New Urban community, with an emphasis on architecture and walkability. The goal of WaterColor, though, was to emphasize the natural surroundings. That was the biggest draw for me when I was looking to buy a home down here."

Having spent time in both communities that weekend, Delia could well see why Max, with his outdoor spirit and affinity, would prefer a home in WaterColor. Both communities obviously had their charms, but, given the choice, she would side with Max. After all, she was a country girl at heart, in spite of having disappeared into city life for a while. A stray thought flitted through her heart. *What might it be like to spend more than a weekend here with this man?*

Delia blushed then quickly ducked her head to avoid Max's keen eyes. His boyish grin told her she hadn't dodged soon enough, but rather than teasing her, he focused on his role as tour guide. As they bowled along, he pointed to the store signs that jutted out from the buildings they passed, highlighting some of the cute and creative names. Soon they were greeted by white stationary umbrellas and a cream stucco building fittingly offset by emerald-green trim. Max slowed and then hopped off his bike to walk them toward the bike rack. Delia and the others soon followed suit.

Palm trees soared from the median while live oaks and saw palmettos layered with pine straw edged the sidewalk of pavers. Bulb lights strung between the palms on the far side of the restaurant made Delia long to return at night for dinner under the stars. A shared look with Max revealed that her dreams matched his own, but the unspoken promise in his gaze concerned her.

Though she wasn't completely aware of his customary work schedule, it was certainly more structured than her own. Careful planning would be needed and more consideration than she usually gave, considering her spur-of-the-moment nature. WaterColor was an easy drive for her, but the same couldn't be said for Max when he was in South Carolina. It could amount to a great deal of time away from his business.

She glanced back at him as he finished locking their bikes and caught a wink from his grinning face. It was as if he had read her mind and was more than ready to remove any roadblocks. Warmed by the knowledge, she tucked her hand into his as he led them to the hostess stand.

Max waited for the others to join them, then asked, "Inside or out? Outside is the best place for people-watching, but inside has a ton of atmosphere."

Anne replied, "I'll let you pick, but I need to freshen up first. I assume there's a restroom inside?"

Max pointed to the far door. "Take that door, and the bathrooms are in the back corner on the right."

Anne returned to the patio a few minutes later as the rest of the group was settling in at a table under the canopy of umbrellas. "It's one stall, girls," she reported with a grin. "That means that Max is going to have to go the bathroom at some point so we can talk about him since we can't all fit in the ladies'!" She flashed a teasing smile at Delia as she pulled out the vacant chair next to Lindsay and across from the man in question.

"I'll be more than happy to, as long as someone puts in a good word for me!" Max answered agreeably as the waiter appeared with waters. He thanked the young man and asked for a bit more time to decide, then turned to the group. "So, I'm sure y'all have more than one question for me, but why don't we get our order in so y'all will have plenty of uninterrupted time for grilling?"

Lindsay shook her head with a grin, her guns spiked. "And don't think you'll get off easy, sir! I'm a lawyer, and I already have a boatload of questions prepared."

"Then I'll use this time to my advantage and fortify myself!" he answered with a laugh and a wink for Delia, who flashed a wan smile. Brow furrowed at her quiet response, he leaned toward her. "You okay?" he asked softly.

Delia glanced at him and nodded. "Just a bit overwhelmed is all. I've never introduced a guy to either my friends or my family." She tucked her head into the menu, slightly ashamed at the emotions that tumbled around in her stomach. *What is wrong with me?* Throughout the service she had basked in the rightness of sitting next to Max in a pew, and yet as they rode with the others following along through Seaside, a niggling foreboding had trailed along like a pesky yellow fly. Now that she was stationary, the doubts began to prick at her.

While she was overjoyed that everyone seemed to be getting along so well, she couldn't help but wonder when it might all disappear. She had yet to tell him about her past, and when she did, she knew there was no guarantee he would still like her. What would she say to her friends if this all blew away like a paper lantern? How would she heal a heart that had been devastated once before?

Max squeezed her knee under the table and leaned over as if to point out an item on the menu. Effectively cutting her off from the view of the rest of the table, he whispered, "It's all good. I know there are things you haven't told me about yourself, and I'm perfectly fine with taking each day as it comes." He paused and ran the back of his index finger down her cheek. "I'm a patient man when I know the end goal, and for me, the end goal is a relationship with you."

Delia sat speechless at his obvious sincerity, tears of relief pricking her eyes as the doubts flitted away. However, those doubts did reveal one truth. He needed to truly understand what he was getting into before she held him to his promise.

~~*

Orders placed and drinks refilled, Max nodded to Lindsay and said with good humor, "Let the interrogation begin!"

Lindsay rested her elbows on the table, hands folded in front of her, and cast him a considering look as if evaluating which of her verbal surgical knives she should use. "Okay then, let's start with the most important and work our way down the list. Are you a Christian, and if so, how long have you been a believer?"

Max glanced at Delia, who flashed a confident smile. "That's a discussion Delia and I have already had, but I'll be glad to fill in the details, and she can judge the consistency of my answers."

Delia took a sip of her iced tea and wrinkled her nose in amusement, her internal crisis seemingly resolved.

"I was raised in the church by faithful parents in a community that has a great deal of faith, but I didn't come into my own separate belief until my father died seven years ago. And to answer your next question, yes, I regularly attend church and a men's Bible study when I'm not traveling, but I've been known to try out churches when I'm on the road. I like seeing the different ways worship is expressed. I've even attended one or two African-American churches, and let me tell you, they know how to have church."

Jess and Anne agreed with his proclamation, while Lindsay nodded thoughtfully as if rearranging her initial evaluation of him. Delia simply gazed at him, a soft, hopeful smile wrinkling her lips. It took all of Max's resolve not to lean over and kiss her soundly. He did allow himself a quick wink in her direction. "What else, Madame Prosecutor?" he asked.

Lindsay didn't hold back. "Tell us about your family. Siblings? Delia mentioned that you run the family sawmill?"

"I'm an only child, though not for lack of trying on my parents' parts. Mom liked to say they stopped with perfection, but I think that was to save Dad's masculinity. They never said, but I got the feeling they couldn't have any more and were lucky to even get me, for whatever reason.

"As I said, Dad has been gone now almost eight years—heart attack at his desk. He and Mom met at community college, and they married not long after. Dad always knew he was going to run the mill when my grandfather retired. He had spent his high school years learning the ropes and didn't want to wait four years of college to officially start with the company. They had just celebrated their fortieth wedding anniversary when he passed.

"I took over from him after working in sales for an international company for ten years." He paused, then added more soberly, "And for the record, I was married in college and we divorced right after graduation." He cleared his throat and glanced at Delia, then said, "No kids."

Delia reached under the table and patted his knee, and before Lindsay could posit her next question, Delia said, "I think that's enough of an interrogation for now. Besides, here comes the food!"

Lindsay backed off with an understanding smile, and the rest of the meal passed in good humor, peppered by Max's tales of carefree escapades on 30A. All too soon, the plates were cleared, the check paid, and they returned to their bikes for the ride back to Betty's house. Jess, Lindsay, and Anne elected to ride ahead, allowing Max and Delia some final private time.

"So, I'm guessing Lindsay is some kind of wonder in the courtroom?" Max asked with a grin.

Delia's brow furrowed in worry. "I hope she wasn't too personal. I did wave her off of further inquiries about your divorce."

Max reached over and brushed the backs of his fingers down her cheek in a soothing caress. "Not a bit, but I do appreciate the consideration. It's not something that I'm proud of, and while I didn't mind telling you, that's different from airing it to the world." They rode in silence a moment as he considered how to ask about her reaction at lunch.

As they paused at the stop sign leading into the park behind the wine bar, Delia tapped his hand and pointed to the grassy area. "Max, let's take a walk." Hearing her sober tone, he expected that she had read his mind, or at least figured his appreciation was an open door to the conversation. They parked their bikes in the grass, and she grabbed his hand as they began to wander through the park.

"There's something I've been needing to tell you. I didn't want to ruin our walk on the beach last night, but today I realized I can't leave without you knowing the whole story." Max remained silent, allowing his support to radiate through his sure grip on her hand. He had had a feeling from day one that there were some murky waters in Delia's past, but he had chosen instead to heed the steady calm of the Holy Spirit as He continued to reassure him that their meeting was God's plan.

After a few moments, Delia apparently decided where to begin her story and took in a deep breath. "It's actually related to how I reacted when we first met." She paused and looked away then bit her lower lip and shook her head, unable to find the words and courage.

Max stopped their amble and turned her to face him. "Darlin', no matter what it is you need to tell me, just say it. Letting it build in your head only makes it ten times worse."

Delia nodded, then dropping her eyes to his chest, she blurted,

"I was horribly bullied as a kid by a boy I liked, and I've never been able to trust guys since then." She shot him a quick, searching look to gauge his reaction. When she seemed to find the support she needed, she continued. "I was an overweight child, and when he learned that I had a crush on him, he tormented me horribly, even saying I was so fat I could eat an entire deli and still be hungry. The awful nickname Deli stuck, and up until we met, that's how I had been known."

Delia took in a breath and then ventured the final explanation for her odd reactions. "So, while I have absolutely loved our time together and most of me knows that you're trustworthy, there's still that little girl who is waiting for you to turn on me—for you to become Jamie and spew cruel insults." She shrugged in helpless bewilderment. "I can't explain why that feeling is still here, even after all these years and the therapy I had in college, but there it is."

Empathy washed through him. This quiet vulnerability and history of rejection and torment meshed with his own life experiences in a way he never would have imagined but for God's hand. Max tucked a finger under her chin to raise her eyes to his. "That was a horrible experience, and I don't doubt that it left a huge impact. Thank you for telling me. It'll help me understand when things trip you up." He raised his other hand and brushed away the tear that had begun a slow progression down her cheek.

"But you have to know that I am not that boy, and the absolute last thing in the world I want to do is hurt you." He paused and lowered his voice, which only increased the sincerity of his words. "I have no doubt in my mind that God put us together this weekend, Delia, and I'm not about to make light of that or neglect it. I have prayed and waited too long for you to come into my life."

A long, shuddering breath slipped through her lips as if her entire being relaxed at his words. A heartbeat later, she was in his arms, her head tucked into the crook of his neck. Minutes seemed to expand to hours as they stood together, and Max silently prayed for God to comfort this woman he was even more sure would someday be his wife.

~~*

Volvo packed, beds stripped, and kitchen cleared out for the cleaning crew, Lindsay, Jess, and Anne sat on the porch, waiting for Delia and Max to return. A smile twitched Lindsay's lips as she asked the others, "So, should we send out search dogs?"

Jess chuckled. "I can track her on my phone if need be."

Anne leaned forward in her rocking chair to peer down the street. "I think I see them. No, never mind. They turned off on one of the other streets."

Lindsay set her own rocker to moving and sighed, "Well, at least there's no hurry to get back. Not that I blame her for taking all the time she can. I never had to do long-distance with John, but I can remember when we first started dating; it was all I could do just to go to class!"

Anne chuckled and was about to add her own comment when she spied two bicyclists heading directly for the house. "Here they are," she murmured to the others, not wanting her voice to carry and potentially embarrass the lovebirds.

"Hope y'all haven't been waiting long," Max said as he held open the screen door for Delia a few minutes later.

Jess grinned and shook her head, "Oh, no, not a bit." Her light tone forewarned that Delia was in for quite a bit of ribbing as soon as they were on the road home.

"We're all packed and ready to go," Anne added. "It was such a pleasure meeting you, Max."

"The same for me," he agreed. "If y'all wouldn't find it too forward, before y'all get started back, I'd like to pray for a safe journey."

Lindsay's jaw dropped a little at his words. As they each linked hands and bowed their heads, she caught Delia's eye and mouthed, "He's a keeper!"

Delia nodded, an amazed delight lighting her eyes. She mouthed in return, "Yeah, he is."

"Heavenly Father," Max began, "we thank You for Your presence in our lives and the blessings that You have given each of us. I especially thank You for orchestrating this weekend for all us. I ask that You give these ladies grace for their travels back to Fairhope. I thank You for the work You have called each of them to do and ask You to bless everything they put their hands to. May they live You out daily in their walks. In Jesus's name. Amen."

"Amen!" the ladies chorused.

Delia squeezed Max's hand, and as she released it, said to the others, "Before we get on the road, I want to make a pit stop."

Lindsay nodded, and as soon as Delia had closed the door, she glanced at Anne and Jess and put a hand on Max's forearm. "She would probably kill me for saying this," Lindsay began, earnest concern and care strengthening her gaze, "but Delia has been more than hurt in the past. She's been truly traumatized, and if your intentions are anything less than honorable—although everything so far speaks highly of your character—it would be best if you end this before it goes any further."

Max nodded, then placed his own hand over hers in an effort to soothe her concerns. "Lindsay, I appreciate your saying something. It speaks highly of your own character that you care so much for Delia." He paused and looked at each lady in turn as he added, "I can assure you my intentions are completely honorable. Delia already told me about her past—not all of it, I'm sure, but enough—and as I told her, I know in my soul that God put us together this weekend, and there is nothing in me that will not cherish her."

With a quick glance at the door and then toward the car to ensure she hadn't snuck out the back, Max continued in a lower tone, "I'll tell only y'all this, now that she's out of earshot because I don't want to freak her out. I have the distinct feeling that this lady will be my wife at some point. I'm perfectly ready to wait as long as I have to in order for that to happen."

The front door knob turned a moment later, and Delia returned to the porch. She glanced between Max and Lindsay, then paused to gauge the overall vibe of the group. "So, what did I miss?" she asked.

It was obvious to Lindsay that Delia knew she had been the topic of discussion. Max raised his eyebrows. Was she comfortable with all he had said? Did she trust that he was a man of his word? Every fiber of her spirit lay silent, calm, sure, and Lindsay answered his silent query with a slow nod. Yes and yes.

"Ohhhkay," Delia interjected as she glanced between the two of them. "Since it looks like no one is going to let me in on the powwow, I'll just say that I did a quick once-over of the bedrooms, and y'all got everything."

Jess threw an arm around Delia's shoulder and said, "It's all good. Just making sure everyone is on the same page." Amid the confirming nods, she added, "As much as I hate to be the party pooper, I think we need to get on the road. After all, I have my own powwow waiting when I get home."

Lindsay reached over and grabbed Jess's free hand in silent support. She didn't envy her meeting with Mitch, and she prayed that God would provide her the right words. On the heels of that prayer was one for Delia, that God would nurture her budding relationship with Max now that several hundred miles was about to be placed between them. Seeing the shared look between the couple, Lindsay tugged Jess's hand and quirked her head toward the screen door. With final good-byes, she, Jess, and Anne left the porch and headed to the SUV, allowing Max and Delia a final private farewell.

~~*

Max tugged Delia easily into his arms soon after the others had left, and she felt him bury his nose in her hair. "Call or text me when you get home?"

She felt the question and the longing underlying it more than she heard, and she nodded against his shoulder. "Definitely," she whispered, then released the plea on her lips: "Don't forget me, Max."

"Never," he answered, hugging her tightly as if to squeeze his reassurance into her. "And let's look at our calendars soon. I don't want to wait six weeks before I see you again."

"I have to be in Charleston in October to begin the story on a few Southern plantations for Christmas magazine issues."

"Let me know the dates, and I'll clear my schedule."

Delia shook her head, her brow furrowing at the thought of his likely busy calendar going by the wayside. "You don't have to do that."

"No, I don't," he agreed, "but I want to and I plan to."

A slow, pleased smile crinkled her cheeks, and she pulled back just enough to grin up at him. "I think I'm falling for you, Max Andrews," Delia mused as she stared into his green eyes, as if trying to memorize their varying tones.

An answering grin lit his face. "I sure hope so because I know I am for you." He leaned down and set his lips to hers. Sweet promise sang along her senses, at least until Lindsay tapped her horn. Delia shook her head in amused tolerance and reluctantly released Max. "I can't keep them waiting any longer. Jess is heading home to break up with her boyfriend of three years, and the longer I stay, the longer it puts off her telling him."

Max grimaced at the thought. "I understand. Be safe, Delia. I—" he paused, then merely nodded. "See you soon, darlin'."

"Bye," she answered as she turned to head to the Volvo. Delia climbed into her seat and tightened her seat belt, and after a final kiss blown to Max, she turned to settle in for the drive.

"So," Jess began as Delia kicked off her flip-flops for the ride. "Just what on earth did you two find to, um, talk about after we left?"

"It was actually really sweet," Delia answered with a bashful sincerity. "I told him about Jamie and the bullying."

"Really?" Anne asked from her seat in the front. "And?"

"He wasn't scared off. In fact, I got the distinct feeling he likes me even more now."

Lindsay chuckled from the driver's seat. "Yeah, I think we've all got that feeling," she drawled as she tossed a fond wink in the rear-view mirror. "Okay, ladies, next stop: home!"

Chapter 17

Fairhope

Sunday was Anne's favorite day of the week. Her neighborhood always seemed to quietly release its breath, as if taking the command for a Sabbath rest seriously. The air around her seemed at peace, hushed, relaxed. She turned and waved to the other ladies as Lindsay pulled away, then closed her eyes to appreciate the stillness around her. A part of her was somewhat surprised that her house was quiet. Either her family wasn't home yet from lunch after church or her son, Theo, was waiting, primed to pounce. She smiled at the thought, and seeing Ted's car in the garage, braced herself for the latter.

Anne pushed open the door to the condo and called, "Hi, I'm back!" Setting her suitcase on the floor, she opened her arms wide just in time to catch Theo in a bear hug as he raced toward her. *And pounce it is,* she thought fondly.

"Mom! I've missed you lots and lots!"

She squeezed him and kissed his cheek. "Me, too, buddy!" she said with a smile. Anne looked up from his embrace and found Ted next in line. She caught his lips in a sweet, lingering kiss.

"Welcome home," he whispered as they pulled apart.

One arm still wrapped around Theo, she slipped the other around Ted and leaned into him, absorbing his familiar scent and feel. "So glad to be home," Anne murmured. With a final squeeze to each of her men, she leaned down and picked up one of the sacks that had fallen to the floor during Theo's enthusiastic greeting. "Theo, I brought something back for you—"

He grabbed the bag and eagerly stuck in his hand to pull out the pirate costume. "Oh, that's so cool! Thanks, Mom! I'm gonna be the fastest sword on the ship!" Theo jetted out of the room, already practicing his pirate accent as the description of his future exploits trailed behind him.

She smiled warmly at his retreating back, then turned to find Kelsie hanging back by the hall to the bedrooms, just off the kitchen. Her ginger hair curtained her face, shielding her reaction to her mother's return, but Anne didn't need to see her face to recognize the slump in her shoulders. Remorse stabbed at her heart as she quietly said, "Hi, Kelsie. You know, I brought you something, too."

Kelsie shrugged and continued to inspect the sequins on her favorite shoes. "Probably a book or something for school," she mumbled just loud enough for the words to reach Anne and Ted.

Anne glanced up at Ted and silently asked for a minute. He nodded and moved toward the family room, out of sight, but not out of earshot. She was grateful for his quiet support and said a quick prayer before saying anything further. "I will admit that when I first bought your souvenir, it was something you would be studying in science class." She watched Kelsie's shoulders slump even further, twisting the knife in her heart a bit more, but Anne continued through the guilt. "Then, after I spent a lot of time talking with God and some of the ladies, I realized something. I've been too hard on you and, in fact, smothered you."

The curtain of hair fell back from Kelsie's face as she looked up. Confusion tinged with hope lit her hazel eyes. Anne pursed her lips and glanced down at the other bag in her hands then remembered, *Humble yourself...and God will heal.*

"I'm not making excuses, but when I thought about it, I was doing to you what Grandma did to me. Like her, I was doing what I thought was best for you. It's what I knew, but I can see now that it's not right, and I'm going to really work on this and try my hardest to step back. So, I got you this." Anne raised the bag and watched Kelsie cautiously take out the item, slide off the rubber band, and unroll it. Taylor Swift's megawatt smile beamed out from the poster.

Shock flitted through Kelsie's eyes before an ecstatic glow lit them. Tears welled as the girl threw her arms around her mother's waist. "Thank you, Mom!" she mumbled into Anne's chest.

Anne blinked back her own tears as she wrapped her arms around her daughter for the first time in what seemed like a year. She leaned down and kissed the top of Kelsie's head and lay her cheek to rest there, savoring the warmth of the girl. After a moment of quiet, she murmured, "I'll back off and give you space, but nothing will keep me from loving you and wanting the best for you. Can we go from there? Not back to what was, but forward to something different?"

Kelsie lifted her head and pulled away slightly. Wiping her cheek with the back of her free hand, she looked up at Anne and nodded. "I think I'd like that."

Anne squeezed her tightly in response then released her, but placed a staying hand on Kelsie's arm. "I can't guarantee I won't slip back into old patterns. This is new territory for me. So I have a lot to unlearn, but tell me when I'm slipping back. No more silence and shutting me out on your end. We have to talk and be open with each other. Deal?"

Kelsie nodded, then, realizing she hadn't verbally agreed, blushed in embarrassment. "Deal." She turned to head back to her room with the poster, but paused before she reached the hall. Glancing back over her shoulder at Anne, Kelsie murmured, "I love you, Mom."

Anne pressed her hand to her lips and blew her a kiss. "Me, too, Kels," she whispered as the girl hurried to her room. As Anne heard the door quietly shut behind Kelsie, she felt Ted's arms wrap around her from behind.

He tucked his chin on her shoulder and leaned into her. "I am so proud of you," he said. "And I am so thankful that God arranged this retreat."

Lindsay pulled the Volvo to a stop in front of Delia's bungalow and turned around in her seat. "Going to call Max now?" she asked with a teasing grin.

Delia wagged the phone that was already in her hand toward her friend. "Yes!" she answered with a chuckle then sobered a bit. "It's nice to have someone to check in with."

Lindsay offered an understanding smile and nodded. "Yes, it is." She glanced over to the other side of the back seat as a ding came through on Jess's phone. "Mitch?" she asked.

Jess pursed her lips and nodded. She let out a slow breath and grimaced as she read the text.

"Well, it looks like God's timing is a lot sooner than I wanted," the blonde said, words dripping with wry acceptance.

"What did he say?" Delia asked.

"He's going to be at my house in thirty minutes." Jess tapped a few letters into her phone then sent the reply.

His immediate reply raised her eyebrows. "Ohhhkay. This is a first." She showed the text to Lindsay and Delia.

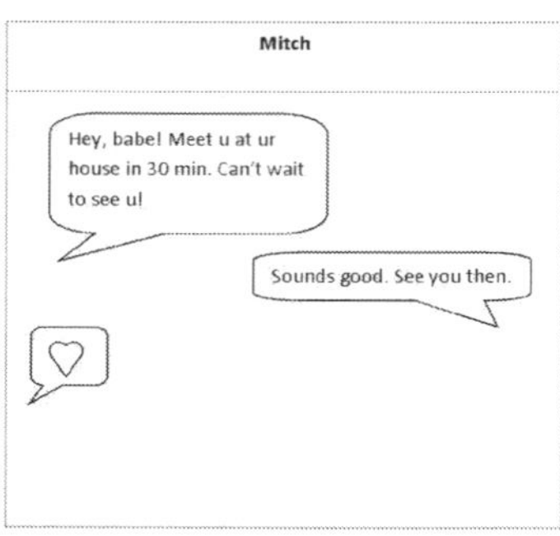

Lindsay found an equally confused look on Delia's face and waited for Jess to explain.

"Mitch has never, in the past three years, sent any type of emoticon in our text conversations, and today he chooses to send a heart?" Jess shook her head. "Crap," she murmured. "Now, what do I do?"

Lindsay reached between the front seats and squeezed Jess's knee. "Guilt isn't peace, Jess. You only do what you have peace about, and trust the Holy Spirit to give you the right words."

Jess nodded and offered a half-hearted smile to her friends.

Delia's phone buzzed. "It's my editor," she said as she glanced at the number on her screen. "I've got to go, but Jess, let us know how it goes, and call if you need to talk." With a side hug for the blonde and the quick admonishment of, "Don't forget Mr. Bubbles," to Lindsay, Delia jumped out of the car, answered the call, and grabbed her bag out of the back. She waved with an elbow as she walked up her front steps, still talking on the phone and dragging the suitcase behind her.

Lindsay shook her head in amusement then shot a questioning glance to the back seat. Jess nodded in response to the unspoken query, and Lindsay put the car back into gear.

Jess pulled the last of her clothes out of the suitcase and tossed them in the laundry basket just in time to hear a brief knock on the front door, followed by Mitch's jaunty greeting, "Hey, babe! You home?"

She picked up the book on Seaside's architecture from her bed and called, "Yes, just in the bedroom. Be out in a minute." Having waffled much of the drive home as to whether or not to give the book to him in light of her decision, she opted to have it at the ready and see how everything unfolded. She had bought it for him, after all, taking into consideration his interests and potential pleasure in receiving the gift.

Jess put it behind her back and joined him in the kitchen. She forced a smile and said, "I've got something for you."

Mitch, however, smiled with pure delight and leaned forward to kiss her on the cheek. "What a coincidence! I've got something for you."

He was so eager and pleased with himself that Jess couldn't bring herself to make him wait and, instead of broaching the topic she had planned, said, "You first."

Mitch's smile widened as he made a show of pulling something from behind his back. Jess's heart sank as she recognized the size and shape of the midnight-blue velvet box. She knew its contents without him saying a word. But then he did speak. "Jess, I have missed you so much this weekend that I realized I didn't want us to spend any more time apart without something to hold onto." He flipped open the lid and pulled out a lovely pear-shaped solitaire diamond ring. With delight in his eyes, he held the ring out toward her and asked, "Jessica Anne McAdams, will you marry me?"

Tears dripped down Jess's cheeks as guilt poured into her. *Oh, God, what do I do?* she prayed.

Mitch seemed unconcerned by her lack of words and instead took her tears as acceptance. He reached to pull her left arm from behind her back. "We can have the wedding whenever you want, but it needs to be after next spring so we can take a honeymoon once the season ends. Unless you want to make the bowl game our honeymoon destination?"

With those words, peace returned to Jess. Her choice and her words were correct. Before he could put the ring on her finger, she shook her head and pulled her hand out of his grasp. "As much as I love you, Mitch, I can't marry you."

Shock and confusion writ on his brow, Mitch dropped his hand to his side. "Why ever not?" he asked. "I love you. You love me. That seems to be the basis for most marriages these days."

Jess closed her eyes against the pain underlining his words and then spoke the truth. "I love God more than I'll ever love you."

She heard Mitch's exasperated sigh and opened her eyes at his retort. "And I've told you I'm okay with that."

"But you can't say the same thing," she answered. Sorrow filled her gaze. She took a fortifying breath and broke his heart. "And I'm not okay with that."

Mitch shook his head in disbelief. "This is about faith again?" he asked, sarcasm lacing his words. He gestured widely, making a peace offering. "Look, I'll try my best to get to a Bible study from time to time."

"It's more than that, Mitch," Jess pleaded, her own heart hurting as she stood her ground, "and I think deep down you know that."

Mitch pursed his lips and glanced away. He took in a deep breath then nodded, apparently accepting what he couldn't change. "So this is it?"

"I'm sorry, but it can't be any other way," Jess said. She raised her hand to cup his cheek. "I do care for you, and I want the best for you."

Mitch let out a harsh bark of laughter and pushed her hand away. "You've got a funny way of showing it," he snarled. Tossing the ring back in the velvet box, he turned on his heels and walked out the front door.

Tears filled her eyes as the door shut softly behind him, its quiet rebuke more effective than any slam. "Oh, God, please let me have done the right thing," she prayed as she gripped the book in her hands. "Let this draw him closer to You rather than make him bitter and angry."

Something stirred in her spirit, and she inwardly heard a voice say, "Don't worry, Jessica. I've got Mitch in the palm of My hand. Release him to Me, and trust the work that I am doing in his life. It's okay to let him go."

Peace flooded through her unlike any she had ever experienced in her life. Jess took in a deep breath and whispered as she let it free, "Thank You, God."

~~*

Home again, Lindsay thought as a sweet comfort settled in her soul. She turned off the engine and sat for a moment, reviewing the last three days. *So much insight. So much truth.* She ached for Jess, but was so grateful for the revelations that God had given each of the ladies and the freedom she had found for herself. Who would have thought?

A light tap on her window jolted her from her musings. John stood just outside, making silly faces at her. Lindsay shook her head at her goofball of a husband and wrinkled her nose at his antics, her wide grin belying any irritation. He stepped back as she opened the door then pulled her into a hug.

"Welcome home, baby!" he murmured into her hair as he squeezed her tightly.

Lindsay kissed the side of his neck in reply then, realizing there were no little ones tugging at her shirt hem, she asked, "Where are the girls?"

"They were having so much fun with Mom and Dad that they begged them to take them for ice cream after church. They'll be home in a couple of hours though." John pulled back from their embrace and searched his wife's face. "But what I want to know is what happened to you?"

Lindsay's brow furrowed in confusion. "What do you mean?"

John cocked his head to one side as he considered her. "There's a light in your eyes that I've never seen before. What changed?"

She shook her head in wonder and let out a laughing sigh. "It was really pretty amazing all in all. I found out that I have been living in fear most of my life. And this decision about whether or not to go back to work is just the latest example. It all goes back to when I told Mom and Dad that I wouldn't be majoring in engineering and I was giving up the GIT admission in favor of Emory."

A curious gleam lit John's eyes. "Really? That's interesting."

"Isn't it? I'm actually still having difficulty wrapping my brain around the fact that such a small thing could have so big an impact on how I thought about and reacted to situations. And the thing of it is, I know if I hadn't gone to the retreat, I never would have heard it." She paused and took a breath, then smiled and said, "But because of that insight, I've decided to go back to work, at least a few hours a week. I'm not sure what I'll do, because it'll depend on what's available, but at least the decision is made, and I have peace about it."

John picked her up and twirled her around in celebration. "Oh, baby!

I am so happy about this. It was tearing me up that you were hurting, and I couldn't do anything about it." He put her back down a moment later, an exuberant smile radiating from his lips. "Then this means I have great news of my own!"

"What's that?"

"Remember I was able to get in a round of golf on Saturday while I was waiting for the last data I needed for the presentation?" At her nod, he continued, "Mark, one of the other guys in the foursome, works at Johnson McGee and mentioned they had just gotten a big contract case and needed both of the partners focused on it. He said they were looking to hire another attorney to pick up some of the slack, but didn't want someone right out of law school, because the clients they handle require finesse and a greater depth of knowledge than a newbie would possess. He actually brought up your name and wondered if you might be interested in taking some overflow—not big stuff, but the little things that fall through the cracks from time to time. I told him I would ask you, and he said the job is yours if you want it."

"What? Are you kidding me?" Lindsay asked, astonished by God's perfect timing.

John shook his head. "Not a bit. Mark said it would be a feather in their cap to have an attorney of your caliber join the firm, even part time."

"Wow," she murmured with a shake of her head. "'How great Thou art,' indeed."

John grinned and released her to move to the back of the SUV and pop open the hatchback. "Well, well, well," he said in a teasing lilt, "I see my admonition to Anne fell on deaf ears!"

Lindsay joined him at the back and peeked over his shoulder at the mounds of bags atop her luggage. "I did get you something," she replied meekly. She reached around him and pulled the T-shirt out of the Trading Post shopping bag and held it up.

John burst out laughing. "I love you," he finally managed around the guffaws.

"Forever and ever, amen," Lindsay answered with a grin.

Chapter 18

Monday morning dawned bright and beautiful, the beginnings of autumn's cool feathering the air. Jess had battled her sheets and comforter as second and third guesses and images of a certain diamond ring pricked at her resolve. Rather than continuing her standoff with dreamland, she got up and dressed and watched the sun as it rose over the tree line. The view was lovely from her front-porch rocker. There was something reassuring in the parallel of sunrise to the newness of God's mercies.

The sun now headed on its regular passage through the sky, Jess glanced at her watch. It was six forty, and she didn't have to be at work until eight thirty. It would take her all of fifteen minutes to finish getting ready, and she wasn't hungry enough to use the time to cook a full breakfast. She contemplated the still-wrapped breakfast bar in her hand and tried to decide what to do. Given the change in the weather from recent weeks, she opted for an impromptu walk down toward the pier with her ultimate destination being the park, which had trails and benches that were perfect for quiet contemplation. The retreat had birthed a longing within her for continuing the reflection and meditation she had learned.

Decision made, she returned inside to pour her morning coffee into a travel mug. She tucked the breakfast bar in the pocket of the windbreaker she would likely need as she reached the pier, and set off to meander and think.

Jess paused as she closed the wrought-iron gate behind her and glanced fondly back at the picturesque setting of her house hidden among the hardwoods. She smiled at the tinges of red and orange that had begun to kiss their leaves. Fairhope was, in her opinion, prettiest in the fall, although spring definitely ran a close second.

She turned to start off on her perambulation, her feet leading her down the street toward the Andersons' former home, the sale of which had apparently closed while she was away, given the lack of a realtor's sign. A contractor with a backhoe on a trailer attached to his truck had pulled alongside the front of the house, and a scruffy, white-shirted man with a well-worn ball cap shading his leathery face stood talking with another man who sported a dress shirt, khakis, and a hardhat. The second man held a rolled set of blueprints in one hand and gestured to the house and the trees that surrounded it.

Jess surmised that someone other than Mitch had won the build contract since she was fairly certain he had put in his name for consideration. She hated that he'd lost out on the job, but decided it was probably for the best. Fairhope was a small town, and while they would likely run into each other from time to time, seeing Mitch daily at a job site just down from her house might be too hard on both of them.

She caught a quick bit of their conversation as the breeze blew in just the right direction to snatch their words and send them her way. "They want to make sure all of the trees stay, so be careful when you start demo."

Jess was relieved that the new owners, regardless of the style of house they built, were at least cognizant of their surroundings and the importance of maintaining the vegetation. The Fruits and Nuts district was known not only for its street names that honored both indigenous trees and fruits as well as the city's founders and their utopian ideals, but also for the mature greenery that hugged houses and sheltered parks.

A few of the Bradford pears and water oaks had begun to shed that greenery; their leaves created a comforting crunch under her feet as she continued toward the pier. She paused at a crosswalk, took a sip of coffee, and grimaced at how quickly it had cooled in the travel mug. It was definitely not one of the Yeti tumblers Mitch would occasionally bring over and leave. However, it was the first of the little things she would now miss in her life.

~~*

Delia readjusted the headset for her new wireless, retractable earbuds as she stretched a bit before her run. The headset had been a gift from Haven for the write-up she had completed the previous month. It had arrived in her mailbox while she and the other ladies were in Seaside. She had been curious about how it would work on her run and had pulled them out that morning rather than her traditional earbuds. A quick pairing of the Bluetooth to her phone, and soon her "Run" playlist was piping in her ears.

About a third of the way down Church Street and before she crossed Fels, the phone rang with an incoming call. Unable to see the number from her armband, she felt around the necklace for the right button and answered as professionally as her breathing rate would allow, "Delia Preston."

She stumbled as Max's smooth low-country accent drawled in her ears. "Mornin', darlin'." Her already short-of-breath lungs hiccupped as she answered, "Hey, good morning!"

"What are you up to?" Max asked, bemused by her tone.

Delia smiled as she paused at Morphy Avenue while a car turned back onto Church. "Just going for my run down to the pier. And trying out this awesome Bluetooth headset a cruise line sent me for writing the article about their newest ship." Car now on its way, she returned to her even pace. "How's the sound?"

She heard Max chuckle as he said, "Crystal clear," and continued along Church, passing the old K-1 Center and community park, which would soon be overrun with kids bused from the elementary and intermediate schools to enjoy recess and PE on the grounds.

"So, what's up?" Delia asked.

"Well, I wanted to check in with you and see if you knew when you'd be heading to Charleston yet."

Delia paused at St. James and took a sip from her water bottle, then answered, "I'm still waiting to hear back from two of the tour guides, but it's looking like I'll be there mid-October, probably beginning the thirteenth, unless these two only have availability earlier in the week. I'll have to get back to you on the definites later. How does your schedule look?"

"There's not much I can't move that week. I have a weekly managers' meeting Monday and a sales meeting Friday, but Tuesday through Thursday should be pretty quiet. The next week gets a little dicey since I have to go to Virginia to meet with our large-volume treaters."

She turned onto Fairhope Avenue, the park now dead ahead just a few blocks away. "Sounds good," she puffed, then fell silent, unable to think of anything to say to continue the conversation.

Max seemed content to listen to her breathing and was silent as well. After a moment or two, he asked, "So, I don't mean to be forward, but what happened with your friend who was breaking up with her boyfriend? Jess, was it?"

Delia grimaced at the memory of the group text conversation they'd had with Jess Sunday night. "It went about as well as could be expected." She paused at the corner of South Summit to fill Max in on the details. "Jess is mainly concerned about his faith and what will happen to it since that was the reason she broke up with him. I'm sure this won't improve his appreciation of God, and I'd be surprised if he goes to church on Sunday, given that he went only because of her." With a quick swipe of her forearm to her brow to clear the beads of sweat that dotted her forehead, she picked up the pace once more.

"That's tough."

"Yeah," she answered, and the silence stretched. All Delia heard was her breathing and footsteps, but oddly enough, it was comforting just to know he was on the other end of the line. She continued down Fairhope Avenue, her pace still even, but her breath a bit ragged. Knoll Park, one of the last bastions of the Sand Hill Long Leaf Pine Forest, was up ahead on her right, but it was the familiar figure huddled on a bench that caught her attention. "Hey, um, can I call you back later?" Delia asked, her voice wavering with uncertainty.

Concern laced Max's answer. "Um, sure. Everything okay?"

"Oh! Yeah," Delia answered, brightening her tone. "I just think I see Jess up ahead in the park and—"

She could almost feel Max's understanding, warm smile over the airwaves. "I get it. Not a problem. Will you call me later?"

"That'd be great." Delia silently calculated her day's activities and factored in the time difference, then said as she slowed to a walk, "How about around seven my time?"

"I'll talk to you then. Have a good day," he said and rang off.

"Hey, stranger! Good morning!" Delia called as she neared the bench where Jess rested, travel mug in hand.

Jess looked up from her brown study of the mug and murmured, "Hey, morning."

Coming to the park that early was certainly out of character for the blonde; Delia had never seen her on her morning runs. Delia settled on the bench next to Jess and took a swig from her water bottle, then glanced over at her friend. A closer look revealed a pale complexion and dark circles under her eyes, both hallmarks of a restless night, which would explain her early presence. However, the unspoken request in Jess's blue eyes for Delia to ignore all these details silenced any comment she would have made.

Instead, Delia said, "I was just on the phone with Max, and we talked about my going to Charleston next month, trying to firm up dates. He asked about you." She offered a sympathetic squeeze to Jess's forearm and watched her lips curl into a wan smile. "Which was sweet," she quickly added. At Jess's nod, she continued, "And then we ran out of things to say. I mean, it wasn't horrendous, but I'm not great at talking on the phone, and unfortunately that's all we have until either one of us is able to travel to meet the other."

"What about writing to each other?" Jess suggested, noticeably thankful for another topic to discuss other than the elephant that had joined them on the bench. "You know, before we had all this technology, people used to write letters to each other. I have some of the ones my great-grandfather wrote to my great-grandmother when he was in World War I that are so touching. You wouldn't have to do the pen-and-paper variety. I'm sure e-mails could work just as well."

A light flickered in Delia's eyes as she considered Jess's suggestion. Writing was more in her wheelhouse, so e-mailing either in lieu of or supporting their phone calls could well be a viable compromise. Max, given his chivalrous nature, would probably enjoy trading love letters—or whatever they would be called at that point in their relationship.

Delia threw an arm around the blonde in thanks. She pulled away and took a hard look at her friend. Once more Jess's eyes pleaded for silence. Instead of commenting, Delia simply pulled Jess back into a hug and silently prayed as tears began to outnumber the beads of sweat on her shoulder.

~~*

Tuesday found the hospital's annual volunteer appreciation party at the top of Jess's to-do list, which necessitated a quick run to the local supermarket to order the cake and pick out a few decorations. Normally, the gathering was the highlight of her year. She enjoyed celebrating those who gave of their time and talents to help those who were hurting, but that day a pall fell heavily on her shopping excursion. The leaden feeling that had seeped into the day before had eased with the tears shed both in Delia's arms and later that night on her couch, but the hangover from her crying jags dulled her spirits. Yes, she knew what she'd done was right, but that didn't mean she didn't grieve. For Mitch. For herself. For the three years they'd spent together.

Cake ordered and a few packages of balloons and streamers selected, Jess glanced at her watch. She figured she had an hour to spare before the afternoon staff meeting, so she decided to call and see if Muriel was up for a quick visit. While Jess was at the retreat, the older woman had been discharged home from the skilled nursing facility, where she had transferred to continue her rehabilitation.

Jess had visited Muriel a couple of times at the facility, but the distance between it and the hospital was too great to allow for a good visit on Jess's lunch break. By the time she would get there in the evenings, Muriel would often be in bed after an arduous therapy schedule. Muriel readily agreed to her suggestion of a quick drop-in, stating her physical therapy would be just finishing up by the time Jess arrived.

A half hour later, Jess had a front-row seat for Muriel's therapy session. As Muriel began her final walking routine with the home health physical therapist, Jess glanced around the living room. The interior of the old colonial off of Blue Island Road had always made Jess wonder if the décor had come with the house when Muriel had purchased it with her husband as newlyweds. The tables laden with doilies and lamps topped with boudoir-worthy shades as well as the Victorian parlor sofa where she now sat harkened back to an era more frequently seen in antique malls and flea market booths than in twenty-first-century living rooms. None of it really suited the Muriel that Jess knew. Jess assumed Muriel's décor would be much less fussy and feminine.

Not much later, the therapist settled Muriel in a wingback chair near the settee and placed the walker within easy reach. Jess was pleased at the progress the older woman had made since she had been transferred home that Wednesday. When she'd last seen her at the nursing facility, Muriel had been able to walk only a few feet before needing to sit down in the wheelchair that followed behind her. Just now, she had circled the living room three times and had to pause only once midstride to catch her breath. It wouldn't be long before she was back leading the Bible study.

"Ah, me," Muriel said as she leaned to one side and pulled the hem of her housecoat out from under her ample frame. "Thank you, Mike. Same time Thursday?"

"Yes, ma'am," replied the tall, lanky man of indeterminate years. "I'll be here. Now you just remember to work on your exercises tonight and tomorrow, and we'll see if we can't change them up a bit on Thursday."

"I will do my best. Have a good afternoon!"

"You, too," he answered with a nod for Jess as he closed the front door behind him.

Muriel turned an expectant look at Jess. "So, tell me about your retreat. What did you learn about reflection and meditation?"

Jess recognized the older woman's tactic. In true Southern conversational tradition, she had opened their visit with an innocuous topic and would wander her way around to her greatest curiosity. Instead of taking the byway Muriel offered, Jess leaned forward, propped her elbows on her knees, and said, "I learned a great deal, but the most important discovery was my peace."

Muriel's surprise was evident. "Do you mean with your young man?"

Jess nodded, a sad smile twisting her lips even as acceptance filled her gaze. "I realized that God had been telling me all along that it was time to let Mitch go and leave him in His hands."

"Well, I can't say that I'm surprised, my dear," Muriel murmured. "I would watch y'all from time to time in church, and it was obvious that there was fair gap between y'all in terms of faith. I was wondering if you would overlook it and floor it to the altar or drop the checkered flag and part ways."

Jess smiled at the euphemisms, in spite of the pain. "I have to say it wasn't an easy decision. Mitch is a wonderful man, and I'm sure most other women would think I am an idiot for letting him go—"

"But a lot of those women wouldn't have your faith and need for the man to be at least open to growing his." Muriel leaned back in her armchair and sent Jess an appraising look. "You know, I always got the feeling Mitch wasn't open to growing."

Jess shook her head. "No, he wasn't. He told me once early on that his parents had dragged him to church as a child and never taught him there was more to it than ritual and good behavior." She sighed at the lost opportunity. "My greatest prayer now, though, is that the breakup won't drive him further away from God."

Muriel reached over and patted Jess's knee. "God knows the end from the beginning. He knows where Mitch ends up. Who knows, it might be back by your side after all. God is the worker of miracles and doesn't want to lose a single one of us."

Jess smiled wanly at the thought and let loose of it as quickly as it moved through her ears. It would do more harm than good to latch onto a stray hope, not knowing if reconciliation was God's intention for her and Mitch. It could easily keep them both from growing and would definitely increase her heartache. "Tell me about you and your recovery," she said, redirecting the conversation to firmer ground. "I can see you're making great progress!"

"Well, it's nice being home," Muriel answered.

"I'm sure," Jess agreed. "Are you okay here by yourself?"

Muriel nodded. "Home health sends a nurse aide twice a week to help me with showering and such, and the ladies in church have set me up with a meal delivery. I tell you, I have enough food to feed me a month over just in these few days since I've been home."

Jess's gaze sharpened at the words. "Please tell me it's the right food, Muriel, or you could be right back where you were."

The older woman chuckled and shook her head at the irony. "I thought I would be getting all of my favorite dishes. After all, I had just been in the hospital. One would think that would warrant a little coddling. But not these gals! June got the bright idea to ask that dietician from the hospital what I should be eating—turns out she's the daughter of a friend—and danged if she didn't give them a list of all this healthy stuff, the majority of which is some shade of dark green!"

Jess laughed, her concern eased. Having worked in health care for so long, she knew how well-meaning friends and family could do more harm than good with their offerings for the recovering patient. With that worry alleviated, she turned the conversation to more general items of interest, including Muriel's request for a recap of the retreat.

Wednesday evening, Anne pulled a roast out of the Crock-Pot and poured a couple of cans of green beans into a pan on the stove. Kelsie sat at the kitchen counter, science book open and pencil in hand. She sighed, tapped the pencil, and flipped the page back, then put her head in her hands with a groan. "You know, Mom," she said, irritation lacing her tone, "right about now is when you'd step in and do it for me."

Anne glanced over from the green beans, which were just beginning to brown, and replied with a sympathetic smile, "You're right, but now I'm stepping back, remember?"

Kelsie's aggrieved wail filled the kitchen. "I didn't think you meant with homework!" she protested. "I just thought it would be with all the other stuff."

Anne chuckled at her daughter's put-upon tone and turned the green beans down to simmer. She wiped her hands on her apron then joined Kelsie at the counter. With a squeeze to her shoulder, she said, "Talk it through with me, and let's see what's going on."

Lindsay tapped the steering wheel as she sat in the parking lot of the law firm of Johnson McGee on Friday morning. She was fidgeting, and she knew it. There was absolutely no reason for her to be nervous. John said that his golfing partner had told her the job was hers to accept or decline. That made this meeting more of a formality than a true job interview. She also knew that God had set this up for her. He had walked her through her breakthrough in Seaside, and He had arranged the position to become available for just this time.

She took a fortifying breath and opened her car door. A short walk up the sidewalk followed by an easy push of the front door, and the familiar feel of a law office greeted her. Polished mahogany wainscoting lined the waiting area walls, and behind a large desk sat a smiling receptionist ready to be of assistance.

Lindsay straightened the hem of her suit jacket. That simple reflex of muscle memory banished the remaining butterflies as a sense of rightness whispered through her. Head held high, she confidently nodded to the receptionist and said, "Hi, I'm Lindsay Davenport."

"Yes, welcome, Mrs. Davenport!" the receptionist returned warmly. "Mr. Johnson is just finishing up a conference call and will be with you shortly. Would you like something to drink while you wait?"

Lindsay shook her head, unwilling to risk the possibility of needing to go to the restroom in the middle of the meeting. While she was confident, she was also well aware of potential pitfalls that could trip her up.

A few minutes later, a tall, angular man with a gray receding hairline and a blue Brooks Brothers suit walked out of an office just to the left of the reception area. A wide grin and outstretched hand greeted Lindsay as she rose.

"Lindsay, so wonderful to meet you. Lawrence Johnson. Please, join me in my office." A firm handshake and gentle touch to her back as he turned them toward the door he had just exited radiated respect wreathed by Southern chivalry. Lindsay immediately felt at home.

"I have to tell you," Lawrence began as they settled into the tufted leather armchairs in front of his desk. "McGee and I were ecstatic when Mark told us the news you might be interested in coming on board a few days." He paused and steepled his fingers, offering her a considering look. "However, I do have to be up front."

Lindsay felt the first stirrings of foreboding at his tone and braced herself for what was to come.

"This case has grown larger and more detailed than we anticipated when we took the client on. We're going to need you to handle discovery with Mark as well as pick up any new domestic work that comes along.

All that to say, we're going to need you full time. Is that going to be a problem?"

Lindsay inwardly blanched. Full time was much different from what she'd had in mind. She rapidly rearranged her expectations in light of the new information and compared them to the family's schedule. Dot would probably be willing to get the girls to dance a few days a week after school. On the days that John was working from home, the girls could ride the bus, and she could be home by dinner. She would make it work. She pulled her lips into a confident smile and answered, "That should be just fine."

As Lawrence proceeded to outline the basics of the breach-of-contract suit the firm had just taken on as well as salary and benefits, the ramifications of returning to the workforce after so many years of absence began to sink in. Lindsay had kept up with her CLEs to keep her license current, but this was a very different arena from state litigation. She would need to come up to speed quickly in order to be an asset rather than a hindrance.

A bit of her concern must have leaked through her professional mask, as Lawrence's smile softened. "Don't worry about being out of the loop, Lindsay. From what I know of your track record and dedication to the law, it won't take much for you to brush up your skills. That's part of the reason McGee and I wanted you to assist Mark with discovery. As you get more comfortable, we'll send new domestic clients to you. This will be a win-win situation."

Lindsay relaxed and pushed any niggling doubts aside. She couldn't wait to tell John the good news.

Chapter 19

Sunday morning, Jess turned on the coffee pot, pulled out two mugs, then went back to the bathroom to shower and dress for church, just as she had for most every Sunday for the past three years. Halfway through putting on her makeup, Mitch would usually knock on the door and then let himself in, pour their coffees, and turn her TV to a news station. This Sunday, though, when she returned to the kitchen, dressed and ready to leave, there was no commentary blaring about the state of the world, no coffee with cream and stevia waiting on the counter. But most of all, there was no Mitch.

She stared at the still-full coffee pot. "I don't know what I expected," she murmured to the mugs, and she reached to put one back in the cabinet. "I knew he wouldn't be here this morning." A tiny part of her still hoped that she might catch a glimpse of him in church. She was certain he wouldn't sit in his usual seat beside her, but surely she wasn't the only reason he attended services. "Right, God?" she asked, her heart pleading against the truth found in the empty coffee mug on the counter.

"I still wish you would have told me that this turned into a full-time position before you took it," John said as he buckled into the driver's seat of the Land Rover, ready to drive the family to church.

"And as I said when we talked that afternoon, it happened in a split second," Lindsay answered, irritation tingeing her words. "There was no way to pause and say, 'I need to check with my husband before I can agree'—at least not without sounding like I was asking permission." The last phrase she murmured under her breath. Better that than upset the two sets of prying ears in the back seat.

Lindsay felt rather than saw John's grimace. "Look, this is a tremendous opportunity," she said. "They're willing to work with my schedule so I can be home for dinner. Dot said she could take the girls to dance twice a week, so we'll just leave off the third afternoon. I'll still drive them to school in the mornings, and they can ride the bus home the other three days since you'll be there."

"What about when I stay late at the base?"

"Lawrence assured me that I can leave early every so often, and I can put off my start date for a couple of weeks if needed, so you can get settled working from home on the days when your mom can't get them. This is going to work, John. It may be an adjustment for a little bit, but it's going to work."

John sighed and then turned to face her. She smiled confidently and ran her fingers down the side of his cheek. "It'll work," she whispered.

He nodded, placed his hand over hers, and planted a kiss on her fingers.

"Daddy, we're going to be late for church! I don't want to miss my class," Abigail piped up from the back seat.

John glanced back at her and blew her a kiss. "Don't worry, pumpkin. We're heading out now!"

As he put the SUV in gear and backed out of the driveway, Lindsay silently prayed, *Please, let it work, God. Please, let me find myself again.*

"Oh, good," Anne murmured as she pushed open the door to the church. "Delia's here." She waved to the ebony-haired woman where she stood getting coffee on the other side of the lobby. Out of the corner of her eye, she saw Theo scamper off toward children's church with Kelsie following behind, heading to the youth service.

Ted squeezed Anne's hand and said, "I'll get Theo checked in so you two can plan." He had been sympathetic, but not completely surprised by Jess and Mitch's breakup and fully supported Anne's thoughts on how to help Jess get through the first service without him.

"Thanks, honey," she replied and walked in Delia's direction. "So, have you seen her yet?"

Delia took a sip of her coffee and shook her head. "No, but I haven't been in the auditorium, so she could already be in there."

Anne nodded. "I'm guessing you haven't seen Mitch either?"

"No. Did you expect to?"

Anne sighed. "No, but I had hoped he would come—if nothing else, for Jess's peace of mind. She's sure that he only attended because she came."

"And I'm sure she's right," Delia said with a rueful shake of her head. "It's a shame, but what can you do?"

The redhead nodded. "So you'll take her out to lunch after church?" she asked. The pair had hatched this plan the night before through texting after Delia had asked Anne about their usual Sunday schedule.

"Yeah, anyplace but a sports bar," Delia commented as she took the last sip of her coffee. "Why don't we head in? If she's not here now, she soon will be."

~~*

Jess stood at the end of the aisle of her customary Sunday seat, bulletin in hand. She stared at the fourth seat from the end and knew it would be unoccupied from that Sunday on. "Oh, God, please let me have done the right thing," she prayed.

Jess closed her eyes against the threat of the tears pricking them. What had seemed like such an easy decision in Seaside now seemed almost cruel, given that she had been the one providing Mitch his faith. She jumped when a pair of hands squeezed her shoulders.

"He has to find his own way," Anne whispered from behind her. "Trust that God knows what He's doing. It's a hard lesson to learn, believe me, but you can't feel responsible for Mitch and his choices. You'll keep him and yourself from growing."

Jess leaned back into Anne's strength and felt a hand grip hers. "We're here," she heard Delia murmur, "and we'll walk with you through this."

The blonde nodded, then, as the worship band began its introduction, she moved into her seat, Delia following behind and then scooting around her to take Mitch's seat. Anne and Ted settled into their usual seats to her right. Surrounded by her friends and comforted by God's presence, Jess squared her shoulders and with calm confidence joined the worship leader as he sang, "It is well with my soul."

Chapter 20

Monday morning brought two new e-mails into two different inboxes that, unbeknownst to either recipient, would have a tremendous impact on the upcoming months. Lindsay had left to take the girls to school while John had finished breakfast then walked upstairs into his underused home office. They would use that week to work out the kinks in his schedule before adding her new work hours into the mix.

John set his refilled coffee mug on the desk and booted up his computer. He clicked his mail icon then waited for the new messages to download. Taking a sip of the coffee, he scanned through their subjects as they began popping up on the screen. There were a few spam e-mails; no matter how he filtered his work account, they always found a way in. Then there were work-related e-mails to read.

Tucked between a note for a free cruise and a request for a review of documentation was something different. He clicked to open that e-mail, curious as to its contents. At first glance, it was a simple congratulatory message on the success of his presentation, but a second reading revealed undertones that held the promise of enormous possibilities:

> John, pleased with the presentation. Analysis on point and timely. Expect to hear from Rear Admiral McGregor's office in the next month.
>
> Michael Brevard, Captain, USN

John pushed back from the desk in his home office and sent his chair spinning, elation rushing through his veins. Hands raised over his head, he whooped and hollered down the stairs, "Hey, Lins! Guess what I just got?"

There was no answer. Nine forty-five. He figured she was running errands after dropping the girls off at school. He reached for his phone to dash off a text, then decided this news was best shared in person. She'd be home soon enough, and they could celebrate all of the doors that were suddenly being opened.

John gave his chair another quick spin and with childlike glee relished the feeling as the room spun around him. He couldn't wait to see what God had in store for them next.

~~*

Jess unlocked her office door, flicked on the lights and the computer, and dropped her purse in the bottom drawer of her desk. Making a mental note to run down to the cafeteria to grab a latte before it stopped serving breakfast, she logged into her computer and clicked on her mail icon. A minute's wait updated the folder with everything that had happened in the hospital administration-wise over the weekend.

Although they were always staffed on the weekends and holidays, it was usually a skeleton crew on the management side. Every once in a while she, too, would work a weekend, just to ensure everything ran as similarly as possible to the regular work week. Unfortunately, she was occasionally met with a variety of unpleasant surprises. She knew that she was due to check on her weekend volunteers before the month was out. After she finished her e-mails, she would look at the schedule for Saturday.

After a minute or two, her inbox quit adjusting for each new e-mail. One e-mail, with red exclamation points and all caps in its subject line, begged to be read first out of the twenty that awaited her attention. Answering its unspoken plea, Jess obligingly clicked on it to reveal a formal invitation.

> Gastroenterology Associates of Fairhope welcomes to their practice Ashley Armstrong, MD. Please join us for a meet and greet on Thursday, October eighth from eleven a.m. to one p.m. at the Doctor's Lounge of The Hospital at Fairhope.

Interesting and welcoming, Jess thought. That practice had long been a bastion of masculinity when it came to their physicians, and Jess had wondered if they would ever add a female to their ranks. She made a note of the time and date, eager to meet the new doctor and begin the groundwork for a positive working relationship. She clicked through the rest of her e-mails and then opened her presentation software to create the flyers for the volunteer party.

As the program opened, her mind drifted back to Anne's whispered words of encouragement before Sunday's church service and Delia's likely not-so-impromptu invitation to lunch afterward. Jess was grateful for their care and concern and was sure she wouldn't have made it through the day without their verbal and physical support.

She was single now. It was a new journey, filled with opportunity and adventures. She prayed that God would guide her footsteps on this uncertain trail she now walked.

In her heart, she knew He would.

Discussion Questions

Chapters One Through Four
Although Anne, Jess, Lindsay, and Deli are all around the same age and have a deep commitment to their faiths, these seem to be the only things they have in common. How do you think their friendships were formed and, more importantly, how are they maintained? How are their friendships similar to your own? In an age where tearing other women down is celebrated, how do you see these characters building each other up? How can you do the same for the women in your life?

Chapters Five through Eight
Think about the women's present and past relationships. How are they similar to your own? What are the moments you're proudest of in your relationship with your spouse or significant other? What trials have you experienced in your past or current relationships? How have each of those impacted your growth as an individual and/or couple?

Chapters Nine through Eleven
Have you ever reflected on Scripture? What were your experiences or insights? Does reflecting on your life events in relation to Scripture change your perspective? If yes, how? How can you incorporate reflection into your daily walk with God?

Chapters Twelve through Fifteen
What are your concerns about meditation? Does Mary's teaching alter your views on it? How did God speak to each of the women through their meditation activities? What change would you need to make in order to incorporate meditation into your own Bible study and devotions? Think

about the women's relationships at this point in the story. How are they changing? What impacts do you think each will feel when they return to Fairhope?

Chapters Sixteen through Twenty

Everyone has had to do something they didn't want to do. Delia doesn't want to leave Max and Jess doesn't want to confront Mitch, but each knows it is the right option. When have you had to do something you didn't want to do? How did you prepare for it? Was the outcome what you hoped it would be? Why or why not?

Thinking back over the book, with which of the four main characters do you most identify and why? How do the women's past experiences impact their behaviors in the present? What issues from your own past still influence your present reactions and decisions? What are some steps you can take to make positive changes now?

Made in the USA
Lexington, KY
10 April 2017